# EMOTIONS:

## The Controlling Factor in the Church

By Russell J. Snyder

Michele –
May God richly bless
you and may your emotions
be found leading you to be like
Jesus in all you do.
Russell
1 Kg 8:61

Contact Information
Wholehearted Devotion Ministries
Email: wholehearteddevotion@gmail.com
www.wholehearteddevotion.com

TXu 1-587-151


www.xulonpress.com

## EMOTIONS:
### The Controlling Factor in the Church

# Table of Contents

Acknowledgements:

I want to acknowledge the people of Village Chapel who have faithfully stood with me on our journey of following after God with our whole hearts. It is a journey that so many start yet like the parable of the seeds find it difficult with all that comes at them in their lives to finish. These faithful ones have been a source of great encouragement as individuals who agree: "I want to be like Jesus".

Dedication:

I want to dedicate this book to my wife Bonnie and our daughters Ashley and Erica for always loving me, even when the lessons of this book were being learned together. Our family means more to me than anything else. I thank God everyday that He has brought each of you into my life, for the lessons we have learned about controlling our emotions during the easy and the hard times, and especially for your sharing your lives with me. I love you.

# Chapter 1

# When Did Emotions Become So Controlling?

Americans have attempted for a number of years to scare themselves to death each year by riding roller coasters, going to scary movies, or doing something that is dangerous just for the fun of it. We prove this by our spending hundreds of millions of dollars a year on these activities which allow our emotions to go crazy. Many would say they participate just for the fun of it, hoping to find some kind of adrenaline rush. It is fun they are seeking. What people experience on an amusement park ride is their hearts beating at what feels like 9,000 miles per hour and their ears hearing screaming at the top of their lungs and finding it hard to breathe themselves. This allows them to exit with a feeling of "being alive." This emotional rush so many pursue, whether they realize it or not, is a product of fear.

Have you ever wondered when emotions became such an important part of our lives? Everyone has them to some degree, whether we are aware of them or not. There are people who act like they have no emotions, yet they do. They may be able to suppress them in some way, but everybody has emotions. Our society is enthralled with them. Emotions regulate us, overrun us – they are the controlling factor in our society and in so many in the church.

They dominate people's decision making. Just think about the decisions you made this week. Why did you make them? What motivated your decision making? Was it because God wanted you to make a decision, or was it because your emotions had impacted your decision? Fear is one of the motivating factors behind so many of the decisions that we make. People buy security systems because they are afraid. They want to be protected. Certain cosmetics are pushed on television and bought in stores because of the fear of looking older. While we may be able to hide it well, everyone will grow older.

There are a couple of reasons the decision to remove swing sets from school playgrounds has been made by so many School Districts. The first reason is because many parents are afraid that their child might get hurt. I sometimes wonder how many children have been swinging on a swing set and jumped out of the swing into the sand or dirt without getting hurt. Were you one of them? The second reason swing sets have been removed from most school playgrounds is the fear by School Districts that they will be sued if the child injures themselves.

In the last half century, emotions have risen in importance to become one of our chief cultural values. The simple phrase – "How does that make you feel?" is one of the greatest examples of this rise in emotional awareness.

Many people are living in depression or despair today. Depression and despair are emotions that are a condition of one's heart. Another example of run away emotions is seen by how many people are being referred to anger management classes because they have allowed their anger to take over in their lives. Anger management doesn't overcome the anger, it just manages it. God wants us to be able to overcome our emotions so we no longer are controlled by them.

Emotions are controlling our society more than anything else. They are used to manipulate people. If you are upset with a politician you may send them an email, call them or do something that often uses a threatening manner to tell them to do what you want. This process involves using emotions to manipulate them, capitalizing on their fears. How people feel is at the heart of many of our societies politically correct decisions. Worriers, voters, first time parents, all are being manipulated by fear. Christians, Muslims, Jews, New Agers, even bigots think emotionally in some way that impacts the manner they choose to make their decisions.

People have even been known to use manipulation in the most benign ways, with grandparents. We can see children and even adults use their grandparent's emotions to convince them to do something they were not intending to do. As small as buying their grandchild ice cream, to persuading them to give up their retirement money so their children and grand-children can spend their grandparents hard earned money in selfish ways. Everyone is impacted by their emotions.

Nielsen ratings reported in a January 23, 2008 AP article that NBC Nightly News is the number one rated news show of the three major networks. When you watch NBC Nightly News everything they report appears intended to stir up America's emotions. The manner in which they report details is intended to stir up people's emotions.

In an article by TV Week on November 11, 2007 "The Today Show" was the favorite television morning show. They too are typically reporting stories by someone who is tugging at the heart strings of viewers. Even the way they report medical information is intended to make you feel like they care more about your health than any other television show.

In the Northwest where I live, somewhere in the first six or seven news stories there generally seems to be an animal involved. "This dog was lost but they found him." Even though there were probably dozens of dogs lost in the Northwest. This one made the news and is inserted into the programming to tug at our hearts because if we feel good about the story, we will keep watching their news program.

The news industry uses ethnocentrism, sensationalism and emotionalism to scare you into thinking you want to know something so you will stay tuned to see what is going to happen. People have been trained to tune out the facts and repercussions of a news story unless it pulls at their emotions. The facts are not as important as getting the emotional response. The news reports go so far as to include people talking about why they think the story happened and how it impacted their city, even when it happened in Nepal. It seems most news reporters look for some tie directly to the city where the watchers live so we can feel part of the story.

Emotions have taken control of us. You see extreme examples of emotions when people riot. You see it in rebellion and terrorism. Just yelling at somebody for what has been perceived as being done wrong. For instance when someone merges in front of your car, you convince yourself it was done on purpose. The windows of our cars are rolled up so our reputations are not ruined as we tell them what we think of them as they drive by, and there go our emotions again.

So often today trophies or medallions are given to every child who participates in a sport whether they have won first place or not. Why is that done? So they will feel good about themselves. We hold graduation ceremonies for pre-schoolers so both the child and the parents can feel good about themselves.

Sometimes we have expressions of encouragement that we give people we work with so that they will know that we think they are making a good effort for a job they are actually being paid to do. What happened to the day when people made a good effort to do their job simply because they were paid to do it without having to be given a Starbucks gift card or some other little extra perk? While appreciating encouragement, do you see how emotions impact every part of our daily lives? It seems we are not in control of our emotions anymore, they control us.

Emotions are seen in physical and sexual abuse. They are seen in crimes of passion, which is why people call these crimes of "passion". People use sex to release emotions because they have confused feeling good physically with actually loving someone. People argue with people instead of having a discussion when their emotions have risen up to such a level they can no longer control their passion about a subject.

All of this begs the question, "What are emotions and where did they come from?" Since creation our emotions have been a part of who we are, how we respond to our environment and to other people. The Bible says that each person has a soul. I believe our emotions are part of our soul. Emotions are a part of our soul, often spoken of as expressions of our heart.

People say things like, "With all my heart . . . .," "from the bottom of my heart . . . .," "my heart is breaking . . . .," "the anguish of our heart . . . .," "the depth of our heart". Emotions are the expressions of our hearts and emotions are the immaterial part of us that have such control over how we think, why we do things and what we say. Matthew 12:34-35 tells us to be careful what we store up in our hearts. Jesus said, "How can you who are evil say anything good? For out of the overflow of the heart the mouth speaks. The good man brings good things out of the good stored up in him, and the evil man brings evil things out of the evil stored up in him."

In Matthew 15:15-20 Jesus makes the point again. The religious leaders have been talking about why Jesus' disciples did not fast and these leaders are offended by Jesus' answer. When the religious leaders became offended by what Jesus said it meant their emotions had taken over. Jesus asked His disciples, "Are you so dull? Don't you see that whatever enters the mouth goes into the stomach and then out of the body? But the things that come out of the mouth come from the heart, and these make a man 'unclean.' For out of the heart come evil thoughts, murder, adultery, sexual immorality, theft, false testimony, slander."

These cannot all be thought of as only actions. Take a look at the words Jesus was speaking about. Evil thoughts are coming from desires and things that should not be there. Much of the time murder is an emotional reaction by somebody. Whether it's because someone is very angry with another person and they hate that person or whether it is because they want retribution – it is an emotional response by someone. Adultery is tied up in emotion. So is sexual immorality of any kind.

When somebody steals something – that too – has an emotional basis. It's as though they are saying "I have to take care of my family so I'm going to go steal this," or "I've got to steal this because I *feel* like I need it." Whatever it is that is stolen, there is an emotion behind their action that has driven someone to steal. You may ask, "What if they are just hungry?" The emotional response to that hunger is, "I have to eat, my body has to have something – and I'm choosing not to find food any other way." False testimony and slander are also found in this verse. Why do people slander others? They want to make someone look bad. Often this will make the slanderer think they look better, and ultimately cause them to feel better. Somehow by tearing down others, people believe they will accomplish what they want.

Joel Garreau wrote an article he gave me permission to quote from entitled, "His Heart Whirs Anew: Peter Houghton Has a Titanium Ticker. He's not sure How to Feel About That." http://www.washingtonpost.com/wpdyn/content/

article/2008/08/11/AR2007081101390.html?referrer=email
articlepg. In this article Joel Garreau said:

"Peter Houghton is grateful for his artificial heart. It
has saved his life. He's just a little wistful about emotions.
He wishes he could feel them like he used to. Houghton is
the first permanent lifetime recipient of a Jarvik 2000 left
ventricular-assist device. Seven years ago, it took over for
the heart he was born with. Since then, he has walked long
distances, traveled internationally and kept a daunting work
schedule.

"At the same time, he reports he's become more 'cold-
hearted' and 'less sympathetic in some ways.' He doesn't feel
like he can connect with those close to him. He wishes he
could bond with his twin grandsons, for example. 'They're
8, and I don't want to be bothered to have a reasonable relationship with them and I don't know why,' he says. He can
only feel enough to regret that he doesn't feel enough...
There were just these few nagging problems in the recesses
of his soul. 'My emotions have changed. Somehow I can't
help that,' he says. He is a Jungian psychologist."

In spite of the incredible gift of a new heart his emotional
response to life had changed. The emotions you have, as well
as your passions, all relate to who you are and what in turn
has been stored up in your heart. If part of your heart is physically changed, this article seems to suggest, your ability to
respond emotionally changes too.

All of this leads us back to the question, "Do we know
where emotions come from?" In Genesis chapter 1 we can
find the answer to this question. In verses 4, 10, 12, 18, and 21
the same phrase is used in each verse. "And God saw that it
was good." The word for "good" is a Hebrew word meaning
it is pleasant or it is agreeable. In these verses "good" is an
expression of God's emotions. People need to know that God
has emotions. In verse 25 the writer of Genesis says,

"Then God said, 'Let us make man in our image, in our likeness, and let them rule over the fish of the sea and the birds of the air, over the livestock, over all the earth, and over all the creatures that move along the ground.' So God created man in his own image, in the image of God he created him; male and female he created them."

The word for image in the Hebrew means resemblance. God placed within every one of us a resemblance of who He is. The word for likeness means in His shape, form or a pattern. You and I are patterned after God and part of our being created in God's image includes our emotions, because God has emotions. We need to know up front that emotions are not a bad thing. God gave you your emotions. You have to understand and realize that in the midst of everything this book brings to light, emotions were given to you by God. When emotions are used correctly, they reveal the image of God in you to a world that needs to see God.

In chapter 2 of Genesis, verse 8 says, "Now the LORD God had planted a garden in the east, in Eden; and there he put the man he had formed. And the LORD God made all kinds of trees grow out of the ground — trees that were pleasing to the eye and good for food." The phrase pleasing to the eye refers to an emotion of God. It speaks to the expression of a desire.

Throughout the Old and the New Testament God's emotions are revealed. In Psalm 103:8 the Bible tells us the Lord is compassionate, the Lord is gracious; He is slow to anger, and abounding in love. Those phrases all speak of God's emotions. When God told Jonah to go to Nineveh he was to tell them they were sinning. Unless they changed God was going to destroy them for their rebellion against Him. Here we see another example of God's emotions. Jonah eventually obeyed and the entire city said, "We need to turn back to God." God relented and forgave them because of His compassion displayed to those who repent.

In John chapter 11, Jesus had gone to see His friend Lazarus who had died and been put in a tomb. John 11:35 says, "Jesus wept". Jesus the Son of the Most High God, the exact representation of God, had emotions and He still does. When God's vengeance is seen in the Old Testament and when God's emotions are revealed because of how people have acted throughout the New Testament, we need to realize that our emotions, our heart's response, is part of what makes up in us the image of God. It is good to have emotions as long as they do not control a person. Somewhere there was a shift from controllable emotions to emotions that we just let run amok. Do you know where this started? In Genesis chapter 3, verse 1.

"Now the serpent was more crafty than any of the wild animals the LORD God had made. He said to the woman, 'Did God really say you must not eat from any tree in the garden?'"

Do you know what emotion the serpent is playing on in this passage? Doubt. It may not be thought of as an emotion, but it is. Doubt is an expression of your heart. It is why doubt can emotionally wreck people. A person can be so sure of what God has done. Then a circumstance of life will happen and they begin to doubt God. They may doubt His love, doubt He cares for them, or doubt He provides for them – it's an emotion. That was exactly what Satan knew was going to take place. So he began to taunt the woman with it.

Continuing on in this passage the woman said, "We may eat fruit from the trees in the garden, but God did say, 'You must not eat fruit from the tree that is in the middle of the garden, and you must not touch it, or you will die.'"

And Satan said to her, "You are not surely going to die are you?"

She probably responded, "Hmm, I don't know." Then doubt began stirring up all kinds of other emotions in her heart.

He said to her, "For God knows that when you eat of it your eyes will be opened, and you will be like God." That was where envy entered in, and jealousy came knocking at the door of her heart – Wow! This is when those emotions began to stir in her until she allowed her emotions to cause her to make the wrong decision. She took the fruit; she saw that the fruit of the tree was good, (it's the same word from Genesis 2:9 where God saw that things were good and that they were pleasing). In that moment, desire – which is another emotion, took over. Ever since then human beings have been struggling with keeping their emotions in check.

There are good expressions of emotions that are incredible examples of God's image in us. Please do not think that this book is about beating up on people's emotions. That is not the goal of this book. The goal of this book is to bring to light how so much of our lives are controlled by our emotions instead of our emotions being controlled by what God wants.

How do we know how to deal with our emotions? How do we know how to treat people when our emotions rise up within us? Follow Jesus' example. Be encouraged by reading the gospels of Matthew, Mark, Luke and John. Look closely at Jesus' emotions and how did He treated people. Each of us should want to be like Jesus, we should want to treat people the way that Jesus treated and continues to treat people. We should want to be more and more like Him, not just in character but in everything He did and in everything that He does.

God has control over His emotions. He still experiences them according to the Bible but He controls them, they don't control Him. In our society we let our emotions control us; seemingly we have just turned them loose. We should want to be like Jesus who always did what He saw Father God doing. He acted correctly on the emotions of God. If we stop and think about it, we know that our emotions are constantly sparring with our mind and our will to do things. We can see this when we hesitate to obey God by asking ourselves, "What will people think?" Most of the time in our minds we know what we are supposed to do, even in our heart we know what we are supposed to do, yet our emotions tend to spar with the thoughts of whether we should do what God wants.

During a Worship Celebration when you are encouraged to come forward and you think, "I don't know if I should do that." Your emotions are sparring with your spirit to keep you from responding to what God wants you to do. There are other points in your life when you have stood there about to do something, knowing it was something you were supposed to do, yet your emotions kept you from acting. Whether it was fear, pride, anger – you figure it out, but know that it was an emotional response that you had.

We ask ourselves, "Should I do this? How will it make someone else feel? How will it make me feel?" Emotions can affect every area of our lives. We allow emotions to lift us high above our circumstances or drag us down because of our circumstances. Whether the situation we are in seems dark with despair or bright with hope we often allow our emotions to impact our decisions.

There is a wrong question we are asking these days and there is a right question we should be asking. The wrong question is "How does that make you feel?" because God does not ask how does that make you feel. The right question we should be asking is, "What does God want me to do?"

How does that make you feel implies however a person is feeling, whatever their emotional state is, should be validated as legitimate simply because it is an emotion they are experiencing. There was a lady who was trained through a

Northwest nursing program to embrace everyone's emotions as legitimate. Once while we were talking about the different perspectives that people had regarding an issue we were discussing at the time she said, "Well, that's their emotions, that's how they feel about it and that's legitimate." When a child wants something a parent is not willing to give them and they throw themselves on the floor and they begin to cry and scream, is their emotion legitimate? Do you want to validate that emotion by saying, "You know what, that's just how they feel." Yet that's what we are doing in our society, with adults as well. What about those adults who feel they have the right to share their emotions because they feel these are legitimate emotions, after all that is how they feel? A lot of the emotions we are feeling should be held back. Instead, by expressing these emotions we are simply demonstrating we are not able to control our own emotions.

The phrase "How does that make you feel?" has even elevated the level of our emotions above spiritual truth. An emotional decision is the primary reason people do not do what God wants them to do. When our emotions validate what we feel we often do even what the word of God tells us not to do. After preaching from the Sermon on the Mount a few years ago, a number of people told me that even though Jesus taught His followers to turn the other cheek; they were teaching their children to defend themselves by pushing or hitting back. They saw their training of their children as how to protect themselves. In making that emotional determination those people were saying "I don't care what Jesus Christ, the Son of God, said and taught, I'm going to teach my child to do the opposite." Though our emotions may not be the correct response, our society teaches people to let them rule in any given situation.

The right question is "How does God want you to live?" If we are living the way God wants us to live, our emotions will be trained to follow. Then they will be able to be expressed the way God wants them to be expressed. But if your emotions are out in front of you, when you want to do what God wants, they will often mislead you.

Someone once said, "If a person misled me as much as my emotions have, I would not consider that person a friend." The reason that rings so true is because emotions are not always based on truth. Instead they are based on perceptions. We see something, our perception distorts our reality and our emotions then react to what we have seen. Perceptions do not become reality, they distort reality. Just because someone begins to think something is true because of their perception of someone or some situation does not make it true. People can become convinced of something about a person they hardly know because people allow their emotions to feel one way about that person.

There is a difference between feeling and sensing. Sensing is about discernment, about understanding what the Spirit of God is doing. That is different than what a person is feeling. You can feel good, you can feel tired, your arm can feel sore because of working out at the gym – that is also how you feel. But when asked, "What are you sensing?" now it shifts to a different mindset that is about spiritual issues; what does God want to have happen?

The next time your emotions start to rise up because of something you hear, ask yourself, "What am I sensing?" Then ask God, "What am I sensing You want me to do with this?" Think of the times you have stopped to ask, "How could I have handled that differently?" and you will see many times that emotions were tied up in the decision making. It's not that emotions are horrible, but they have been allowed to rise to a level of control in our lives.

We need to own three truths. The first is we need to surrender our emotions to Jesus because as the Lord of every part of our lives they too belong to Him, not just our body but also our soul and our spirit. We died with Christ, crucifying even our emotions to be like Jesus. Jesus wants us to walk with Him in a way that every area of our lives follows after Holy Spirit. There is a prayer that many use each day. They pray, "Body line up under my soul, soul line up under my spirit, spirit line up under Holy Spirit." By declaring this, Holy Spirit is put in charge over who a person is. If their body gets what it wants, they will not necessarily do what God wants. If their soul steps out from under the alignment described in this prayer and goes after what it wants, then they will not always go after what God wants. Yet when their spirit is aligned with Holy Spirit, their soul and their body is aligned with their spirit. Their emotions will be aligned properly under Holy Spirit's direction because it is through one's spirit that they communicate with God.

As a child of the King, one of our responsibilities is to walk in Holy Spirit (Gal 5:16), following His guidance and direction so we do not give into wrong desires. There are times emotions rush in on children of the King and we realize that is how God may feel. It is at those moments that we recognize the heart of God maybe rising up within us. While emotions are way out of balance in our society, we must realize our emotions are not always wrong, they often are out of balance in our decision making process.

The second truth is that we need to trust Father God, trust our Lord Jesus and trust Holy Spirit, not our emotions. In Genesis 12 Abram was afraid that because he had an incredibly beautiful wife their relationship might cost him his life. So instead of trusting God, he made the emotionally based decision (the emotion being fear) to tell a half truth and say that Sarai was his sister instead of admitting that they were married. This is Abram, whom God had promised through a Covenant relationship that he was going to receive the land, his descendants were going to become a great nation and all the nations of the world would be blessed by him. At this time in Abram's life he had no children. The God of the Universe had shown up to make these promises to Abram and in the midst of this decision, rather than trust God to protect and take care of him in order to fulfill God's Covenant promise, Abram and his wife chose to deceive the Pharaoh of the land. Abram knew that he was going to receive animals and other gifts that would contribute to his wealth if Sarai would follow his lead, and so she did.

The result of Abram and Sarai's emotional decision was that God inflicted diseases on Pharaoh's household because Pharaoh had taken Sarai to be one of his wives. This type of choice still happens today. Many people who have given their lives to Jesus do not trust Him. Somehow, for people who gave themselves to God years ago, doubt has become the controlling factor in their lives. So, when they don't feel worthy of God and His love, they doubt if they can trust Him with their lives.

If you surrender your emotions to Jesus Christ and trust Him you will realize that you need to retrain your emotions because you have died to the life you lived before giving yourself to Jesus. You no longer live in the life that was controlled by sin. When sin controls your life, emotions control your life. But you do not have to live that way anymore if you have given your life to Jesus. Now you have died to that life, you have been raised up with Christ, you are seated in the heavenlies according to Ephesians 2:5-6, and from there you should have a different perspective on your emotions. It falls to believers in Jesus to retrain their emotions and retrain how they respond to their emotions.

Romans 8:5-11 points out that: "For those who are according to the flesh set their minds on the things of the flesh, but those who are according to the Spirit, the things of the Spirit. For the mind set on the flesh is death, but the mind set on the Spirit is life and peace, because the mind set on the flesh is hostile toward God; for it does not subject itself to the law of God, for it is not even able to do so, and those who are in the flesh cannot please God."

While emotions are not evil, how we respond with our emotions depends on whether we are setting our minds on what our flesh desires or on what the Spirit desires. When we respond from what Holy Spirit desires, we use our emotions correctly and we are blessed. Do you see the difference? You can think the way of the flesh that says, "I want what I want," or you can think the way of God that says, "I want what God wants." One leads to death, the other leads to life and peace. Many people today cannot find peace because they are not choosing what God wants for their life.

If you set your mind on what the flesh wants, you are hostile toward God. That hostility may show up in a passive/aggressive manner like what happened to Eve in Genesis 3. When she was told what to do, she did not get angry, yell and scream, she just did not do it. Have you ever met a Christian who just does not do what God wants? They just do not do it. It's not that they do not believe in God, and they would tell you they trust God, but they just do not do what God wants them to do. It is because their mind is being controlled by their flesh or their soul and not by the Spirit of God. It makes sense that if their mind is controlled by the Spirit of God they will do what God wants them to do.

Romans 8 goes on to say: "However, you are not in the flesh but in the Spirit, if indeed the Spirit of God dwells in you. But if anyone does not have the Spirit of Christ, he does not belong to Him. If Christ is in you, though the body is dead because of sin, yet the spirit is alive because of righteousness. But if the Spirit of Him who raised Jesus from the dead dwells in you, He who raised Christ Jesus from the dead will also give life to your mortal bodies through His Spirit who dwells in you."

The key phrase is "if indeed" or "since" the Spirit of God dwells in you. People believe that an evil spirit can come and dwell, inhabit, make its home in or possess a person. In a similar way we should allow Holy Spirit to come and dwell, inhabit, make His home in us. We should be willing to allow Holy Spirit to possess us. Think of how life would be if God's Spirit possesses us – what a change would take place.

If the Spirit of God lives in you, your emotions should align under Holy Spirit and then you will make right decisions based on the Spirit of God, not based on your flesh. Have you ever been shopping and seeing something thought "I can get that!" Then something inside you said, "No, you shouldn't do that." Did you find yourself arguing with that voice saying, "I can make this work." Still the voice within you responded with, "You shouldn't do that." That was Holy Spirit saying you did not need that. Then your flesh or your soul responded, "Yes I do, I need this!" But it should not be about what your flesh or your soul wants, what your emotions are convincing you to get – it should be about what Holy Spirit desires.

We have to retrain ourselves to understand that our lives are all about Holy Spirit and what He desires us to do, so that we can be like Jesus, and we will see what Father God is doing. We are seated in the heavenlies (Eph 2:6). If we see what Father God is doing, we will be caught up in doing what He is doing. But too many times our emotions say, "I know that's what I need to do, but I have all these things I have to do myself." When we give in, our emotions take over again instead of choosing to align with Holy Spirit.

When we align with Holy Spirit, our emotions align as well and good things happen. Wonderful things happen because our thoughts are God's thoughts; our emotions are God's emotions. We obey God and He blesses us because of it! That is the kind of life God calls us to, where our emotions are tied into Him.

You may be asking, "How do I know the difference?" You already know the difference. Galatians 5:11 can be translated: "But I say, walk in *or live in* the Spirit, and you will not carry out the desire *or emotions* of the flesh. For the flesh sets its desire against the Spirit, and the Spirit against the flesh; for these are in opposition to *or in conflict with* one another, so that you may not do the things that you please. But if *or since* you are led by the Spirit, you are not under the Law." (Words in italics were translated and added by the author.)

Then the Bible says, "Now the deeds of the flesh are evident, which are: immorality, impurity, sensuality, idolatry, sorcery, enmities, strife, jealousy, outbursts of anger, disputes, dissensions, factions, envying, drunkenness, carousing, and things like these, of which I forewarn you, just as I have forewarned you, that those who practice such things will not inherit the kingdom of God."

Every one of these deeds is tied to emotional reactions or responses to things. Immorality is desire and lust. Impurity and debauchery, debauchery being out of control partying. Most people who become alcoholics or drug addicted do so because they are trying to hide some emotional or spiritual issues in their life. They are trying to kill the emotional pain.

Every thing has some spiritual issue behind it. Every thing has some spiritual relationship to what we do. If we are not doing what God wants there is a spiritual issue of our heart or our soul and often it is that our spirit is not aligned with Holy Spirit so we have short circuited God's messages to us. Instead when we go off to do our own thing it is like we have sent back one of those email messages to God that says, "Notification failure." God says do this and we send back a notification failure. Sorry God; did not hear you. It must be my computer is malfunctioning. God says, "Yeah, it is and your soul is the computer." The soul, the brain, is supposed to be receiving these things from God through your spirit.

Galatians 5 talked about idolatry and sorcery. Those are issues of trying to use demonic means to control your destiny. When you worship another god, when you put something else as a higher priority than God, then you have stepped into a place where your emotions say, "I desire this more than I desire God." Sorcery is simply trying to control a situation you do not trust God to control. So when someone tries to control through spells, or through rebellion, or through any number of demonically controlled spiritual techniques it is because they are not trusting God. They are trusting another spiritual being they think they are controlling

Instead we should be asking God, "What do you want to do?" and take part in what God is doing without allowing our emotions to control whether we will be a part of what God is doing. All over the world new and creative ways of touching lives are taking place. The emotional response of much of the body of Jesus Christ over the years has been, "We've never done it that way before." Yet God says in Isa 42:9 "Behold, the former things have come to pass, now I declare new things; before they spring forth I proclaim them to you." And in Isa 43:18-19 "Do not call to mind the former things, or ponder things of the past. Behold, I will do something new, now it will spring forth; will you not be aware of it?"

We need to accept the premise that "if you always do what you've always done, you will always get what you have always gotten." So much of the body of Christ keeps doing what they have always done, and they keep getting what they have always gotten. We have to stop saying, "God can't work that way!" Why can't He? Because my emotions say He can't. This God we serve does not really care whether our emotions approve of what He does or not. At some point we have to line up with Holy Spirit and say, "God, whatever

you choose to do, I am willing and I want to be a part of it."
He is going to do new things in people and through people.

He is going to so move in our society that people at the
top of the 7 mountains of influence in our society (family,
religion, education, business, government, media/arts and
science/technology) are born again, Spirit filled believers.
These will be people who God will help to cause what they
know is true to flow down from the top. We have a lot of
people trying to grow their beliefs from the bottom up. It
is time to partner with God and see people He places at
the top of these spheres accomplish great things for God's
Kingdom.

We need Christian public school teachers, we need
Christian politicians, we need people in the workplace as
supervisors, managers, business owners who can impact and
change the direction of business because of the position God
has put them in. The result of this type of business person
is they may end up with a lot of money. Praise God, for the
Lord will use this type of income to advance His Kingdom
if it is the right people who end up with the money. You will
also begin seeing this more and more in the way the Church
takes care of her pastors. Rather than the mindset that says
the pastor should be poor and drive the junkiest cars, the
Church is taking better care of her pastors. And she should!!
God told the people of Israel to take care of the Priests and
Levites in the Old Testament. It has been the spirit of religion and tradition that has manipulated people's emotions so
that the Church has not financially taken care of her pastors.
But tradition and religion pull our emotions back to how we
have always felt taking care of pastors should be done.

There will be some in the Church whose emotions will
cry out against the types of changes I have just mentioned.
They might even call it worldly. But God does not and so we
should not either. Most people have traditions in their lives.
Let me challenge you to spend some time evaluating yours.

Do you hold to your traditions because emotionally it has been comfortable when God would have you let go of them to advance the Kingdom of Heaven? Are you willing to let go of what your emotions tell you are a necessary part of your life? If the traditions you hold to are advancing the Kingdom of God in ways He desires, you should evaluate them to see if there is a new way God has for you, because most of us hold on to traditions primarily for emotional reasons.

Here are 3 thoughts for us to consider that come out of this chapter. First, we have to recognize that we have issues with our emotions. Most people in the world and the Church do not recognize this. Yet our actions will always follow our beliefs. What you believe will dictate what you do. If you believe that Jesus Christ is most important in your life then you will not be afraid to talk about Him. If you feel He is important, but being politically correct is more important, you will not talk about Him. If you believe you should not offend people, rather than share Jesus with people, then you will not risk offending people because you will not talk about Jesus with them. Actions will always follow our beliefs. This is essential to understand – we need to say, "I believe and know that I am able to control my emotions instead of being controlled by my emotions." The recurring theme throughout the chapters of this book will be "Control your emotions or they will control you."

So repeat this out loud because confessing it with your mouth is the first step toward believing it in your heart.

"I believe and know that I am able to control my emotions instead of being controlled by my emotions."

We have to believe that God will help us every time we surrender our emotions to Him. We have to start believing this – that when the emotions start to rise up and God says don't do that – we will trust God that He will help us overcome that incorrect emotional response. Just as He will help us emotionally respond the correct way. Please bear in mind that our emotions often masquerade as Holy Spirit. It is why people who love God do things they should not do. They believe that God wants them to do something that God has no intention of them doing. An extreme example of that would be someone who believes God wants to save lives by not allowing abortion so they go out and kill a doctor who performs abortions. That one who believes in God, may even love God, would not be following the Spirit of God by murdering that doctor. Instead, their emotions masqueraded as Holy Spirit to convince them that what they did was what God wanted.

Galatians 5:22-23 lists the fruit of the Spirit. This passage describes attitudes and actions, not emotions. It says, "The fruit of the Spirit is love (an act of self-sacrifice for the good of another – which we will talk about in chapter 2), joy (an attitude of the heart), peace (which is something God brings to us, our emotions do not work peace up), patience (an attitude that is then revealed in our actions toward people), kindness (is actually doing something good or constructive for someone else), gentleness (is another word for meekness which is strength under control), faithfulness (which is an action lived out based on our beliefs), and self-control (which is the answer to living out our emotions like Jesus did). There are 9 fruit of the Spirit. My wife has told me a number of times that anger is not a fruit of the Spirit. I have looked it up in the Greek – it is not there and she is correct. I have noticed in Ephesians 4 it says be angry and do not sin, so it must be okay to be angry at times as long as we do not sin. We will cover that in Chapters 7 and 9.

The second thought for us to consider is that we have to think differently about our emotions. We have to start becoming more aware of our emotional responses each day. Look for how what others say or do affects your emotional well being. When somebody does something that bothers you and your emotions start to well up realize that when you emotionally give in to that person you put yourself into emotional bondage to that person. Your emotional state becomes dependent on what happens with that person, what they do or say.

We have all heard people say, "He made me do it!" He made you do what? "He made me get angry, he made me throw the ball at him, he made me slap him, he made me...." Then when asked, "How did he make you do that?" The response is usually something like, "Well, he just did." Come on now, weigh your emotions as you begin to feel them rise up, because every one of us are able to recognize when our emotions are rising. Ask God to make you aware of your emotions starting to rise up and then ask God, "Is this you?" If you think you don't hear God very clearly, you will start to if you ask Him these types of questions. God wants you to have your emotions respond the way His Spirit wants them to respond.

When something happens that grieves your heart because it is just wrong, justice isn't being done, and your heart begins to break in a situation, you can be confident this is the Spirit of God. Yet your response should not be, "I'll write an angry letter." Our initial response should be to turn to God and say, "Oh God, you have to change this. You have to move in this area, you have to bring justice to this situation." Your emotions are moving with God in that way. Ask yourself, "How did that make me react?" Not how did that make me feel, but how did that make me react? You may have to do that when you get home and it is three hours later. How many times have you reacted to something and three hours later, or maybe 10 minutes later, you were asking yourself, "Why did I do that?"

Ask yourself, "How did that make me react?" If you even start to justify your reaction, it was emotions that controlled your reaction. If you find yourself saying "Well I wouldn't have done it if . . . ," then you can be sure that is your emotions taking over. "I reacted this way because it demonstrated the love and glory of God to the person in their life." If that is true, then that is God directing your emotions. "I react this way because the person was clearly an idiot and had no sense at all!" Probably your emotions? Of course it is your emotions. Start reacting and responding to people like Jesus did.

How do you know how Jesus reacted and responded to people? Pick up the gospel of Matthew, Mark, Luke or John and read what Jesus did. Do not read it with the "I already know this" attitude. Try reading it and where ever there is an emotional response, put an "e" next to the verse in the margin. Very soon you will have "e's" all over your Bible. You will find that the Bible is full of emotions; some of the emotions good, some of them not good. But it is full of emotions. Do not believe people who say, "You are supposed to control your emotions so that they are not seen at any time." Do not believe that, if you want to be like Jesus, for His emotions are seen all through the gospels. Still, He followed after Father God, so He knew what the desires of Father God's heart were. Father God's emotions are seen throughout the entire Bible. Choose to do what God wants, not what your emotions want.

The third thought is that we have to walk in the Spirit not in our emotions. Start by memorizing Galatians 5:22-23, it is the Fruit of the Spirit. There are nine fruit of the Spirit. Memorize them, put them in your heart, and put them in your mind. Ask for Holy Spirit to fill you each day and let's stop yielding our lives to our emotions and yield them to Jesus instead. Ask Holy Spirit to put a check in your spirit regarding your emotions. I started doing that myself and you know what? He did. There are times that He checks me soon enough that my emotions are pulled back and I realize, "that's an emotional reaction."

One day I found my soul being worked up and every thing that was happening seemed to stir up anger in me. I told my wife, "I don't know what's going on here but everything is ticking me off." When she prayed for me I received God's peace and suddenly things stopped making me angry.

If you let Holy Spirit control you, your emotions will not. You need to take some time and process what has been shared in this chapter. The Lord has been talking to you as you have been reading about your own emotions. Do not be concerned right now about your family's emotions, your spouse or children, your mom or dad's, your brothers or sisters, co-workers, or anyone else's emotions. Be concerned about your emotions and say, "God does any of this ring true for me?"

The first action you need to consider is, if you have never surrendered yourself or your emotions to God, you need to do that. Stop and do that now. Say to God, "I surrender my emotions to you." Then within the next 24 hours find someone to pray with you and say that to God in front of them. Get someone to put a witness on it with you. Determine that you are going to have your emotions line up with God, aligned under Holy Spirit.

Secondly, if your emotions are out of control and you know it, if reading this chapter has been like Holy Spirit has been tapping you on the shoulder, then pray for the 3 thoughts shared in the last few paragraphs to bring change to you. Pray asking God to help you realize that you have issues with your emotions, to retrain your thoughts about your emotions and to walk in the Spirit. At this point it would be a good idea to find someone you trust to pray with you about these things. Jesus said in Matthew 18:19 "Again I say to you, that if two of you agree on earth about anything that they may ask, it will be done for them by My Father who is in heaven."

If you are not in a place where you want to retrain your emotions, if you are not in a place where you want to do what God wants you to do, you should ask God to change your heart so you are willing. Also, follow up by telling someone where you are not in a place where you are willing to retrain your emotions or to do what God wants you to do. Then ask them, "Would you pray for me that I would be willing, just that I would be willing?" God wants to do something amazing in your heart today.

If you are one of those rare people where it is all lined up and your emotions are God's emotions, let me encourage you to make it your daily prayer for God's Spirit and power to impact the emotions of everyone, especially for His Church and those you come in contact with each day. Because when people in God's Church do not get along with each other, it is an emotional response that has to be changed.

Having read this, if you think that I believe that most decisions are based on emotions, you are correct. I believe that the overwhelming majority of issues going on in the world, in your world around you, relate to emotional issues of some kind. It is because people do not walk in the Spirit.

In the rest of this book you'll see how emotions impact us on a practical level as we address some daily issues we face. Yet throughout this book, you'll find practical and biblical ways to deal with your emotions. Remember one thing. You cannot change someone else's emotions, but by the power of God working in you, you can control your emotions. Either control your emotions, or they will control you.

# Chapter 2

# Why Do Emotions Control People Today?

Our flesh and its desires can keep us from what God wants. The flesh is different than the 'old man.' The Bible refers to the 'old man' in the flesh. The 'old man' refers to your spiritual condition before giving your life to Jesus. It was who you were, who others expected you to be, who people trained you up to be when you were dead in your sins. You didn't know God and you didn't have that relationship.

When you gave your life to Jesus you became the 'new man,' who God says you are and who He sees you as, while the flesh is still there. The flesh is the natural cravings and the physical desires of our bodies. The flesh is always fighting with the spirit because the flesh doesn't want to do everything that God wants us to do and that is why our spirit needs to be in tune with Holy Spirit.

It is why we've got to be aligned with our bodies or our flesh under our souls, and our souls under our spirits, and our spirits under Holy Spirit, because the flesh constantly doesn't want to do what God wants us to do. Sometimes the flesh just doesn't want to do what we know we need to do? Mowing the lawn? Does your flesh say, "Yeah, let's go do that?!" When somebody says, "Take out the garbage," do we say, "I'm into that 100%!" When the alarm clock goes off, does your flesh say, "Get up, get up! It's a great day!" Or does it say, "What, that can't be now?" There is a constant struggle that goes on within us, and when sin or emotions or both are in control, we just don't always do what God wants.

Why do emotions control people today? Emotions control people because we're surrendered to our emotions and not to the Lord. We surrender to whatever we feel like at the moment. In the traumas of life emotions can be wounded. They can make a person susceptible to yielding to untruth, to lies, and to perceptions that distort reality in the future. Look at that statement one more time. In the traumas of life, and everybody goes through traumas of some kind, our emotions can be wounded by what happens around us, or to us, even to other people. They can make a person susceptible to yielding to untruth. I know that God loves me, but the untruth is that He does not care. That can make us susceptible to lies, flat out lies that are told to us.

Somebody may say something to us and we emotionally decide to believe it, even though we know it is not true. We may begin believing perceptions that are going to distort the future. We may begin to think, "Well, I'm never going to be happy, I'll never be blessed, I'll never..." and we buy into those thoughts with our emotions. Because we have come into agreement with our emotions, we begin to look at all of life through that perspective. Rather than reminding ourselves of what God says is going to take place, our emotions keep dragging us back to believing thoughts we know God has said are not true.

We can be healed from the traumas of life and we can be healed of those kinds of perceptions about our future because God wants to change them to help us understand how good He is, what He has planned for us and how much

He plans to bless us. He wants to tune our emotions in to Him so that when He moves, we immediately act upon what He's doing because we desire to do it. You see, emotions include happiness.

Being surrendered to your emotions is a stronghold. Strongholds are strongly defended places in your life where your emotions control how you perceive what happens to you. They are the mindsets you have that cause you to be defensive when somebody else calls you on them because your emotions are in control of how you see and react to life.

If you're a person given to anger, then whatever happens to you, you are sure that someone did it on purpose causing you to perpetually view life through angry lenses. If you are a person whose emotions are tuned in to God, then no matter what happens, you find a way to praise God for it. You will be able to say, "You know what, I'm still going to praise God. No matter what happens, I still know that God has what's best for me, because He loves me and He takes care of me. Emotionally I'm going to respond God's way rather than a different way."

Your strongholds can give you a negative view of life or if your strongholds are in Jesus Christ you will see life in a positive way. Through out the Psalms the Bible calls the Lord the Psalmist's stronghold. As always, the enemy of our souls wants to twist who God is and encourage us to create strongholds that cause us negative views of life. While talking with the Lord I heard Him say "Strongholds are in your lives because your emotions are running amok."

I thought about that and asked: "Okay Lord, what does run amok mean?" My initial thought was of a person trying to run through muddy terrain, ground that was so muddy it is difficult to lift one's feet out of it. That is not at all what run amok means. In reality Webster's Dictionary says the word "amok" means "in a violent or frenzied manner". To 'run amok' means to run around attacking everybody one meets, to exceed all bounds of restraint, to go wild. When there is a negative stronghold in one's life it is because our emotions have run amok. They have gone wild. They are not restrained. They are not controlled by God. We begin to build strongholds around those emotions that are not checked by God's Spirit.

A little five year old had decided in Kindergarten that when he came in from recess he did not want to sit in the circle to listen any more. He threw himself on the floor and began to cry. Now that was emotions run amok. We can look at that and say, "Well, that is a child, of course." Some of us do the same thing. We may be standing up while inside we are throwing ourselves on the floor, because we have learned how to hide our emotions that have run amok better than a five year old has.

Emotions can flat out get out of control. Fear can get out of control and bring anxiety attacks. If you have ever had an anxiety attack, you feel out of control. You just feel you can not hold on. When I was in my first year of full time ministry the leadership board at the church wanted me to work six days a week while they also wanted me to finish my seminary. So, on the seventh day, I was expected to take a class in seminary. We lived about two hours from the seminary I was going to, so Monday afternoon I would drive down the freeway, take a class that was held on Monday evening and Tuesday morning. I was then expected to drive back to go to work. I did that for one semester. I did not have a single day off and in the church where I was, there were gazillions of things going on all the time.

I was exhausted by the end of the Christmas season. Three days after Christmas, at 11:30 at night, I was lying in bed having a panic attack. I had no control over what was going on at all. My wife was asking me what was wrong. If you have ever had one of these attacks, you know the feeling. I called one of our Associate Pastors in the middle of the night. He was older and wiser than I was.

I started to explain to him what was happening and in mid-sentence he cut me off. He continued to explain to me what I was feeling and what was happening. I asked him how he knew what I was experiencing. He explained that he too had experienced panic attacks during this time of year. He had overloaded his schedule. Becoming exhausted, he had pushed himself to the point where he could not control his emotions any longer. Then he told me what I needed to do.

He told me, "You need to quit going to Seminary and focus on the ministry. You're going to take the next two days off." He sent my wife and me down to South Coast Plaza, a large shopping mall in Costa Mesa, California.

He said, "You're going to go down there, you and your wife, and you're going to sit in one of the outdoor café's. You're going to watch all the people walk by. You're just going to relax and not think about ministry or any of your responsibilities. You're going to pull back from everything and get refreshed."

Once I understood that anxiety attacks were coming against me, partly as spiritual attacks, and partly because of my emotional condition, I realized I needed more rest. Then I would pull back and God could do some things to set me free.

Emotions can get out of control. They can be fed like a wildfire and when that happens, they affect our bodies, our minds and every other part of us. Ever wonder if emotions can get out of control, is it possible to be too happy? Have you experienced being out of control happy? I've met people who have looked that way.

In Genesis 37 is the story of Joseph and his family. It says in 37:1 that his father had stayed in the land of Canaan and Joseph (the 11<sup>th</sup> of 12 sons), who was a young man of seventeen, was tending the flocks with his brothers. Joseph brought their father a bad report about them. If you have been in a big family, you know that things can happen in a family when one child became upset at another and it put everything in the family out of balance. A family of two is a big enough family to have that happen too, right? Well, this was a family of twelve boys, and he brought a bad report about ten of them.

I looked up the phrase because I thought, "A bad report – I remember one of my brothers, who was the more righteous one in our family, would periodically bring Mom bad reports about my other brother and me. It wasn't that it was bad in the sense that he was lying about us, but it did mean that we got in trouble for it. So to me, that was a bad report. But that is not what this phrase was talking about.

In this case a bad report means a whispering, defamation, or an evil report. It literally says there, a bad, bad report. The author used the word bad twice. The second word bad means it was evil, it was disagreeable, it was malignant, it was unpleasant, it was displeasing, it was unkind, it was vicious. So Joseph, number eleven of twelve, comes back to his Dad, and whatever he said was not good about his brothers. And the phrase implies that it was not that they were doing something wrong, he just went off on them to his Dad. He slandered them or as our young people would say, he ripped on them.

His brothers viewed him as a tattletale and nobody likes a tattletale. The word "tattletale" means one who reveals something. Already, you have to realize that something was wrong in the family. Emotions were stirring. We know the brothers could not have been happy because Joseph had given a bad report.

While this was going on the Bible added that Israel, or Jacob their father, loved Joseph more than any of his other sons. Do you think the brothers might have known that?

Joseph had been born to Israel in his old age. Israel had made a richly ornamented robe for Joseph, and he had given it to him. When his brothers saw that their father loved him more than any of them, they hated him. They could not speak a kind word to him because their emotions had run amok.

Why do emotions control us today?

Sometimes it is the circumstances that come into our lives and we respond a certain way. But no matter what the circumstances are, we don't have to let our emotions get out of control. In this case, they were so mad and so angry with him; they couldn't see anything nice about him at all. I do not know if you have ever been in that position. It's a horrible position to be in because you keep adding more fuel to the fire of your anger. The anger never goes away. You've found somebody who has so disrupted your life that you have nothing good to say about them. The emotion grows into this hatred, this rage toward them.

Joseph had a dream and when he told it to his brothers; they hated him all the more. He said to them, "Listen to this dream I have." He talked about them binding sheaves of grain in a field, there they all are, when his sheaf stood erect and their sheaves all bow down on the ground to his sheaf.

His brothers asked him, "Do you intend to rule over us? Will you actually rule over us?" They were not saying this because they were happy with him. They hated him all the more because of his dream and what he had seen. His dad loved him and they hated him.

You know why his dad loved him? Without taking you back all the way through the entire story, in Genesis chapter 30, it tells how his dad had wanted to marry a woman named Rachael. But because of some deception by his future father-in-law he ended up having to marry her older sister, Leah first. Then he married Rachael. So, he was married to Leah whom he did not love as much as he loved Rachael.

They started having children, actually Leah started having children. His other wife, Rachael, was not able to have children. Rachael decided that she was going to give her maid to Jacob so she could have children for her. Leah stopped having children, so she gave her handmaid to Jacob as well. All of a sudden he had four wives; two of them technically he was married to, the other two were what we would call common law wives.

Finally, the Lord remembered Rachael and listened to her. God opened her womb allowing her to become pregnant. The first son she gave Jacob after the other ten had been born was Joseph. That's why Dad loved him more than any of the other sons, because he loved one of his wives, Rachael, more than the other three. Now, I am not in any way condoning parents loving one child more than another, I am just telling you what happened. The emotional reaction of Joseph's brothers was severe. The young man was seventeen years old and their father was lavishing more on him than he was on the others. They were basing all of their unhappiness on year's of believing the statement, "that's not fair."

This is an emotional reaction, an emotional response that people have all the time. It's just not fair. You may be one who says, "My dad didn't love me, I couldn't do anything to please him. My dad – was not fair to me." Your soul may have been rehearsing these things for years and you need healing because of the situation with your dad. You may relate more to the brothers than to Joseph in this case. You are never going to be able to control your emotions as long as you give in to them because of what somebody else has done.

As a matter of fact, if someone is constantly angry at somebody else, they are in emotional bondage to them. You may say, "I'm not in bondage to anybody." Yet, you are. A person may have your number even if you don't realize it. When things happen in your life, you will know you are in bondage to them because you will not be able to live your life without being angry at them.

As God so often does, He will put you in a place to test your heart. The Lord did that with both Joseph and his brothers. Do you wonder if Joseph was even supposed to share the dream with his brothers? I am not sure that God told him to share the dream with them. But he did, even though he knew they were ticked off at him.

Joseph had another dream, and here we go again, he shared this one too. His brothers hated him even more, if that was possible. But his father did not hate him. He did wonder if this dream meant Joseph's mother and father, as well as his brothers would actually come and bow down to the ground before Joseph. His brothers were jealous of him, but his father remembered the dream. His dad did not get angry about it, but his brothers did. If you want to know how it ended and how the dreams were fulfilled, read the rest of the book of Genesis.

What needs to be seen is that there were two different reactions to the same circumstances. You may recognize that his dad loved Joseph. Have there been times people have been in your life who you may not have been wild about yet you did not get all angry with them? They may have made decisions you did not care for, and you had to choose how you would respond to them emotionally.

In Joseph's case, it was a classic example of a family and how a set of circumstances erupted in such a way that their emotional reaction was anger, jealousy and hatred. They could not find a single kind thing to say about him. It was not only his fault, but it was also his dad's because of how his dad loved him more than his brothers. Perhaps he could have gone to his dad and said, "Don't ever do that again, Dad." The entire story line demonstrates the need to control our emotions while living in a world where we are taught that however one "feel" is right.

One more foundational basis for what we will be studying. We looked at Galatians 5:16-23, which is the difference between the flesh and the Spirit as well as the listing of the Fruit of the Spirit. In verse 24 the Bible goes on to say, "Those of Christ Jesus have crucified the flesh with its passions and its desires. They have chosen the Spirit of God instead of their flesh." Passions are fervent or excited emotions. Desires which are affections, lusts, cravings or longings are emotions that are related to our flesh and our soul. God is saying if you are of Jesus Christ, then you crucified the flesh and your passions and desires with Jesus. That means they do not have to control you anymore. It means it is your choice not to give in to those emotions. God's power is available for you to change the way you respond to your emotions.

He nailed them to the cross with Jesus. You have said, "I want Jesus' death to take the place of mine so that His death paid for my sins. The old ways I have lived is in contrast with how God wanted me to live, so those ways are nailed to the cross." With them are your flesh and your emotional responses to what the flesh has been influencing. I do not think we get that. I do not think we truly understand that we can choose to follow God's Spirit over our emotions. Then we will do exactly what God wants us to do in that moment.

Since we live in the Spirit, we need to keep in step with the Spirit. This is at the heart of the problem with Christians whose emotions have such control over them today. So many of us do not live in the Spirit and do not walk in the Spirit. We were saved, we might have been baptized and even have a baptismal certificate, but we do not really understand what it means to walk in the Spirit. So we continue to have this struggle with the flesh. In verse 26, Paul said, "Let us not become conceited, provoking and envying each other." Where did that come from? He had been talking about walking in the Spirit, and then in verse 26 he said "Let us not become conceited, provoking and envying each other."

Conceited is the idea of vain glory. It is an emotional response. It is when we think too highly of ourselves. Provoking one another is when we challenge someone to combat or a contest. In other words, when we provoke someone we want to be right at the cost of another person. We see that in the Church today when someone has to be right. It does not matter that the issue they are arguing about will never really have an answer until we get to heaven.

We should remember the only person with perfect theology, that is absolutely correct, is God. The rest of us are trying to understand God and what He wants of us. While God may be sharing revelation with us in the midst of our everyday discussions about life it is often in this situation we see that a person thinks they always have to be right. When this happens that person is provoking somebody else. Rather than letting someone complete a story, we get in an argument over the details of the story, because our emotions rise up and we provoke each other in a contest over whom is right. Paul said not to do that; not to provoke each other by shoving it in each other's faces.

The other word is envy, and that is to want what another person has. He said do not be so high minded about yourself that you think "you're all that", when you are not. Do not provoke other people, and do not look for reasons to push their buttons.

If we had the time I would tell you dozens of stories of people I know growing up and how skilled we became at provoking each other. When we were really good at it, we could provoke each other, get the reaction we wanted, and not get blamed for it. It is what the church does today. We look for ways to provoke others, instead of encouraging each other, instead of using our emotions the way God wants. He wants us to build each other up in order to help us see what wonderful people God says that we are. The Lord wants us to help others realize that they are a son or daughter of God and that He *says* they are "all that'. God says they are incredible people. We have to do more of that.

We have to control our emotions while listening to what another is saying so we can respond the way Jesus would. 2 Corinthians 5:17 says, "Therefore if anyone is in Christ, he is a new creature; the old things passed away; behold, new things have come." We are not who we were, we are who God says we are. That means we do not have to respond emotionally like we always have, we can respond the way God wants us to. Bringing us back to the two choices we have in our lives every day.

Are we going to choose the flesh and do what our flesh wants, or are we going to choose what the Spirit of God wants us to do? Most believers in Jesus Christ have allowed their flesh to control them instead of yielding their lives to the Holy Spirit's control, by giving into the little things. When we give in to our flesh we know that God has something else for us to do yet later that evening we sit home and watch TV instead. We choose to do that even though God has told us He has something for us to do.

Our flesh may be saying, "I'll do it Lord, but I am so tired right now that I just don't have the energy."

While God is saying "I want you to read this book."

"I'll read the book, Lord. I'll finish that book," we respond, "but it would be easier for me to watch this sporting event, to watch this movie first."

What an example of choosing the flesh over God's Spirit. It may be something else. It may be when the Lord tells them to fast, but their flesh does not like fasting. My flesh likes chocolate. When I am fasting or trying to lose weight, chocolate is not one of the essential food groups, but my flesh thinks it is. I can choose what God's Spirit says, or I can choose what my flesh tells me. Some people may say,

"I don't think the Spirit of God really cares about what we eat." Oh, He does. Otherwise, your flesh wouldn't be trying to convince you that He does not care.

When God wants you to do something and you do it, you are choosing His Spirit. When the flesh wants you to do something it is almost always not what God wants you to do. If the flesh is fighting with God's Spirit, then what your flesh wants is not what God wants you to do. How often do you give in? As your flesh fights for something your emotions kick in and justify it. When you do what the Spirit wants there is an emotional response that says, "That is so cool."

It used to be that I always wanted to be on the prayer line because I wanted God to do something; I wanted to be part of what God was doing. But now, as God has people trained up and I'm not on the prayer line, there is a great happiness that comes to me by watching other people do what God wants them to do. That comes with walking in the Spirit. Your emotions, when they are in tune with the Spirit, bring you great happiness. Emotions themselves are neither right nor wrong.

For example, anger is not always wrong. Ephesians 4 tells us to be angry and yet do not sin. So there must be times when it is okay to be in the Spirit and be angry about something.

Emotions are part of the image of God in us and we should realize that we are not wrong every time we respond emotionally, unless we react to our anger without following God's Holy Spirit. Most believers do not live filled with Holy Spirit so they give in to their emotions rather than control those emotions. It is why they can justify being so angry about something when God is trying to show them the flip side of what has happened. If they could see what has happened the way God sees it then their emotional response would be aligned with God's desires.

I may have just made you terribly uncomfortable because I have said that most believers do not walk around filled with Holy Spirit. But they trust their emotions more than they trust Holy Spirit. Sometimes our emotions flat out masquerade as Holy Spirit. People think if they feel okay about anything, then it must be okay to do, rather than stepping back long enough to wait on God until they are sure of what it is that God wants them to do, even if they have felt really good about it. Feeling good about it is different than letting the peace of Christ rule in your life.

For the peace of Christ to rule in your life you have to allow Holy Spirit to be in control of your life. Many believers have been taught to be more afraid of the enemy influencing them than they have been taught to trust that if they ask God for Holy Spirit, Father God will give them Holy Spirit. They also seem to fear being controlled by Holy Spirit because they want to be in control. At the heart of this issue of control is fear. Because fear attempts to get you to doubt and be afraid of what God is doing instead of embracing what God is doing. If you struggle with this, ask the Lord, in the authority of Jesus' name, to make fear leave. Ask God for Holy Spirit to begin to move powerfully within you and take up that place where fear held residence.

Whether you see, listen, hear and obey God is impacted by the flesh, the soul, and the spiritual struggle that tries to overcome God's Spirit. It is the flesh that so willingly gives in to the sin that exists within a person and therefore that individual yields to their emotions. The more one confesses sin when God reveals it, the less they will have a problem with emotions.

If sin is in a person's life, then sin is going to direct their emotional response to so many things. When their flesh is constantly feeding on the sin that is present in their life, the emotions will respond in the wrong ways. The flesh wars against God's Spirit even though a person has become a new creature because the old person had always given in to the flesh. The flesh does not like the fact that you are faced in a new direction and becoming who God wants you to be. It wants you to be the person who allowed your emotions and decisions to be run by the flesh.

You are now saying, "No! I want my emotions and everything to be run by God's Spirit." This is why I say without God's Spirit it is so difficult to control one's emotions. It is almost impossible. When a person walks in the Spirit, they live as a new spiritual person.

I learned a truth from a lady who is 84 years old. We were talking about keeping the family happy. She asked me how to keep the family happy and what came out of my mouth was a response I have often heard and said.

"If Momma ain't happy, nobody's happy."

She responded, "You know whose gotta make Momma happy?"

And I said, "Well, yeah, Daddy does."

"No," she said, "If Momma ain't happy," it is because Momma needs to get happy. It has nothing to do with Daddy, or the children. It simply has to do with Momma's got to learn to be happy in God."

Ultimately emotions must be overcome and trained by you. You are the one that has to be retrained by the Spirit of God. We know that when we are training someone up to do something, they still have to do it, right? There are coaches for every sport, who are training their players up to be the best player they are able to become. The bottom line is this; the player has to play the sport. The player has to work hard and become the best they are able to be. The coach cannot do it for them. If the player does not work hard, there is nothing the coach can do to make them work hard.

If you don't respond to what the Spirit of God says, then your emotions will still be in control. You will never change and become the person God wants you to be. If we can not control our emotions, they bring a hurricane-like windstorm into our lives. They uproot the truth. They devastate hearts. And they cause us to doubt God, His love, His plan and His truth for us.

Life does not come without battles. There are battles in everyone's life. Many battles are small things, some of them are large things and a few of them may seem overwhelming. It is these battles that test our emotional and spiritual strength. Rather than telling God you just want Him to take all of these away, know that battles come to test, strengthen and grow your faith. The Bible says in James Chapter 1, "the testing of your faith produces endurance."

You may feel like, "Man, I'm swamped, I'm under it," much like that TV show called "The Greatest Catch," where they take you out into the Baltic Sea to catch crab. The waves are coming way over the top of the ship and they are almost washing the fishermen away. You may be saying to God "I just can't do this anymore." But those are the times that God strengthens you in your faith in Him to trust Him, instead of running away from Him. It is during these battles that you learn to overcome your emotions. You learn to train your emotions, to direct them correctly so that they do not control you and take you on an uncontrollably wild ride.

Emotions need to be overcome because they can determine our spending patterns. When someone's got financial issues, usually their emotions have somehow taken over their spending patterns. They think thoughts like "I really need this, I deserve this, and I should do this". Emotions can overcome our self-worth by telling us we are not worth anything. Emotions can ruin friendships; they can determine self destructive patterns of life.

Now the good side is that emotions can determine your spending patterns in a positive way. You can say I want to please God, I want to do what He wants, and then you spend the way He wants you to spend. Emotions can overcome your self-worth in the sense that you may have been a person who never thought you were good for anything, but all of a sudden God's Spirit begins to raise you up to see yourself as somebody that is of great value. You begin to appreciate who God made you to be, and your emotions, aligned with God, begin to build you up to the person that God says you are. You will quit believing those thoughts and lies you have been told that have torn you down. You begin saying, "You know what God, You are right, and I feel good about myself this morning." Instead of saying, "Oh God, it is morning," you will start saying "Thank God it is morning, because I know who God has created me to be."

At the seat of our emotions, all too often, our faith will bow or it will yield to the patterns of life. At the seat of emotions our faith bows unless we are in control of our emotions. If asked to pray for a sick person we may respond, "Well, I don't know if I can."

That is our emotions telling us not to pray. It's usually fear. We are afraid we will be rejected or God will not answer our prayers. One of our High School young ladies told her teacher at the beginning of the semester she was the Worship Leader for our Youth Group. Her teacher told her to stand up and sing something. For her to stand in front of 90 sopho- mores and sing the beginning of *Oceans Will Part*, she had to overcome some fear, didn't she? For you to talk to some- body at work, you may have to overcome fear. That is an emotional response and you are doing what God wants you to do. If you ask God, His Spirit will speak through you.

Bonnie and I were talking to some friends about how when people are baptized in the Spirit, and the Spirit of God fills them there is a boldness that comes upon them to start sharing Jesus. Thoughts come out of their head that they did not even know were there. Bible verses that pop up that they learned somewhere, and they share with people what God has done. They may even end up praying with those they are talking to because God's Spirit has overcome their emotions, especially fear. All of a sudden their emotional response is: "Now this is cool! This is good! I'm doing what God wants me to do, and it's all because of the power of Holy Spirit that is at work in and through me!"

The story is told of a man that went to a barbershop one time to have his hair cut and his beard trimmed. He got into a discussion with the barber about all kinds of things. They talked and talked and eventually they touched on the subject of God.

The barber said, "I don't even believe that God exists."

The customer said, "Why do you say that?"

He replied, "Well, if you just go out on the street you'll realize that God doesn't exist. Tell me, if God exists, why would there be so many sick people? Why would there be abandoned children? If God exists there shouldn't be any suffering or pain. I can't imagine a loving God who would allow all of these things."

Rather than give the barber some explanations for this, because of fear he didn't say anything. He didn't know what to say. He was afraid he was going to start an argument. So rather than even get into a discussion he just did not say anything. He let the barber finish his haircut and he went outside. As soon as he stepped outside the door he saw a man in the street with long, stringy, dirty hair and an untrimmed beard. The man looked dirty and unkempt.

The customer turned back, he walked into the barbershop and he said to the barber, "You know what, barbers don't exist."

The barber said, "How can you say that? I'm here and I'm a barber and I just worked on you."

The man replied, "No! Barbers don't exist because if they did there would be no people with dirty, long hair, no untrimmed beards like that guy outside."

The barber tried to explain, "Wait, barbers do exist. What happens is people don't come to me."

The customer smiled and said, "Exactly. That's the point. God too exists, but when people don't go to Him and people don't look for Him, it doesn't mean He doesn't exist. That's why there is so much pain and suffering in the world."

Each of us can step from one moment thinking "I don't want to get into this argument," to another when God gives us some special insight in that moment and all of a sudden we have an answer that God's Spirit has given us we did not have before. Sometimes we become afraid and we do not go to God. We do not look for God. So we forget He is there to guide us.

Emotions are going to determine if we're going to advance what God wants and violently take the Kingdom of God or if we are going to choose to be silent and inactive. When your emotions are in control it helps with the battles. Uncontrolled emotions can cause us to lose the battle or fight, or become overly aggressive in fighting. When you're training up your children, if you lose emotional control, the child wins, right?

If you control your emotions, your emotions won't be manipulated by other people. At the heart of a lot of our problems is reacting emotionally when our emotions are being manipulated. It may be the enemy manipulating how we feel, rather than allowing us to walk in the Spirit so our emotions will line up under the Spirit.

If you think the answer is to turn to psychology; psychology's purpose is to explain behavior, not to fix it. A lot of times psychology will say 'medicate it.' We'll get to that in another chapter. But the role of psychology is to explain behavior. This is why it does not seem to be the person's fault that they are the way they are. Psychology's role is to understand why people do things, not primarily how to fix their behavior. That is why some people go to counselors for years and years and years. If you think I'm saying "Don't go to counselors," please do not take me to that extreme. I know people who have gone to counselors who God has used to work through issues, helping them to come out the other side healed and wonderfully walking with God. I know that is true. There are counselors who do not know God and when people have sought their advice the patients have just become more messed up. If you are going to choose to go to a counselor, make sure to go to the person from whom God wants you to seek help. Be sure they are going to help you work on the emotions that are at work within you.

Often people explain behavioral patterns as syndromes or disorders. The word syndrome refers to a set of concurrent things such as emotions or actions that usually form an identifiable pattern. While watching the Newhart Show a number of years ago, there was an episode about one of the characters named Stephanie Vanderkellen who was always causing problems. One day she walked in to the Inn and announced, "I just came from my shrink."

Bob Newhart's character Dick Loudon asked, "Really, what did she tell you?"

"I have OBD," Stephanie responded.

"What is OBD?" Dick wondered out loud.

"Obnoxious Behavior Disorder, that's why I'm obnoxious," Stephanie explained.

Sometimes when studying people it seems we just want to identify what the problem is without helping change the problem. Rather than say, "Okay, this is my problem," and there are these issues of emotions that need to be dealt with, people instead say, "Now I understand why I do this." But it is not enough to understand why we do it; a good counselor is going to help you understand how to change the behavior by starting at the seat of it with your emotions.

That is why when people have gone through our deliverance ministry, over and over after we have discovered the reason for their behavior, God has shown us how to help the person be set free of their issues. As we would pray in a setting where the Spirit of God was moving and touching people's lives, suddenly the Spirit of God would begin to reveal situations or bring to people's memories the incidences that took place earlier in their life. God would say, "I can heal that, I can take care of that right now. I can heal that emotional trauma that took place in their life." Then each person would have the choice, do they want to be healed, or do they want to continue to do what they have always done?

A disorder is an abnormal, physical or mental condition (Merriam-Webster's Collegiate Dictionary, © 2000, p. 334). Something that is not normal whether it is physically or whether it's mentally – it is a disorder. But if it is a syndrome it's an identifiable pattern (ibid. p. 1192). There are good syndromes, because there are good habit patterns. There are also bad habit patterns that can destroy things. That is why you go back in your life and look at how you emotionally respond to things.

So how do we overcome emotions? Here are four actions you can take. First, you have to take down the walls that your emotions hide behind. You need to confess those things that are protecting your emotions from God taking control of them. Often it is sin or damaged emotions themselves. You have to talk with God and confess the walls to rid yourself of them. You can say, "Lord, I know that my emotions; the panic, the fear, the anger, the desire to be happy in ways that aren't what you want, keep me from taking the walls down which keep me from You."

These are the things that build the walls up and keep us from being healed emotionally and overcoming our emotions. Then you have to renounce them. You need to say to them, "In the name of Jesus, I renounce this control." While reading in the Bible I noticed Ezekiel spoke about this very manner of deliverance. Ezekiel 14:6 says, 'Therefore say to the house of Israel, this is what the Lord says. Repent, turn from your idols and renounce all your detestable practices." Repent, turn and renounce. Repent, turn and renounce. That's what tears down those walls.

Secondly, you have to choose not to give in to wrong emotions. Be aware of your emotional condition and when you know it is a wrong emotion choose not to go there. If you are experiencing the correct emotion then you will realize it is okay and will act accordingly. You're going to have to choose. The way you are going to be able to choose is by surrendering your emotions to Jesus on a continual basis. Not just on a daily basis. On a continual basis you will need to surrender your emotions to Jesus. You will find you need to ask Him through His Spirit to help you know what the correct emotion is and what the wrong emotion is. Then you will be able to respond with the emotions Jesus would.

The third action is to be filled with Holy Spirit. Each day, be filled with Holy Spirit. When you roll out of bed in the morning, ask God to fill you with His Spirit. In the middle of the day you may need to say, "Lord, fill me with your Spirit. God I want Your Spirit to be in control of my life. Obviously, I don't get it right 100% of the time, but Your Spirit does, so Lord I want Your Spirit to fill me."

The fourth action is to change how you think about your emotions. Begin to evaluate your emotional responses. Periodically step back and say, "Did I respond to that correctly?" It is our taking responsibility for wrong emotions that's going to change those emotions. If a person reacts emotionally in a wrong manner, then they need to ask for forgiveness.

You may say: "I reacted in a wrong way emotionally and I don't want to react that way, so I need to confess to you. I need to train my emotions to respond the right way."

You may be wondering, "If I do that, won't they think I'm weird, or won't they hold it against me?" That is your pride saying you are not willing to take action. If we would learn to go back to people when we react emotionally in the wrong way and ask for their forgiveness, we will retrain our emotions up quickly. I cannot think of anybody that wants to keep going back and asking for forgiveness. You need to change how you think about your emotions by evaluating them.

If you find yourself defending why you emotionally responded you should step back to evaluate and say, "Holy Spirit was that really You? Because I'm defending myself and I shouldn't need to defend myself, I should just trust You with these things."

Take down the walls that protect your emotions by confessing them. Choose not to give in to wrong emotions, which means you have to be aware of your emotions. Surrender your emotions to Jesus continually. Be filled with Holy Spirit each day and change how you think about emotions.

Do you really want to nail this down? Take out a card, write down the Fruit of the Spirit in Galatians 5:22-23 and memorize them. If you will start taking action today as you deal with emotions, God will keep bringing the fruit of the Spirit into your life. The Lord will teach you how to control your emotions.

# Chapter 3

# The "Poor Self Image" Syndrome

Do you expect to be the best engineer, the greatest waitress, the most capable plumber or most creative chef? Many a person has stepped into failure by doubting their abilities, lowering their expectations of what they are capable of, or belittling their worth and what they do. Everyone who has a poor self image belittles themselves in some way. They have heard others belittle them and they have come into an agreement with what they have heard. Whether it was based on what they have done, what they do or who they are.

You are worth so much more than you think you are. Some people have settled for being a horseshoe when God wants them to be the balance spring for a watch. While the same metal can be used to make a horseshoe as well as a balance spring for a watch, the balance spring is of much greater value. If you feel like you are just a horseshoe, one of the great things about God is that He can reform you into exactly who He wants you to be. You can choose to be a horseshoe or you can recognize that as a child of the King you are worth so very much to the King. So much more than you think. You are able to see yourself rearranged into who God sees you were created to be.

People are not created with a poor self image. They are not born with a poor self image. God created you in His image and God does not have a poor self image. If you have bought into this poor self image syndrome and are wondering why you feel the way you do about yourself, then let's look at God's Word together and discern some of the reasons why you may be struggling with this.

Syndromes occur when emotions or actions occur at the same time usually forming an identifiable pattern. People have a poor self image because their emotions are interacting with actions and words that have or are taking place with which they have come into agreement.

If you hear phrases in your heart and mind like "I could never . . . ." You need to replace those thoughts with "Nothing is impossible for God." Impossible is an opinion it is not a fact. God wants to take your life and help you realize that there is so much He has for you. He wants to work in you and through you. As long as you keep stepping back and saying, "I'm just a horseshoe," then that is all the value you will see for yourself. Your self image will be poor.

When you step into who God says you are, He strips you of that mental image and He makes you into someone who sees yourself as incredibly valuable. It is your choice even if you do not believe it has been your choice. It is your choice because by the power of God you can be transformed.

Self image is an emotion based picture of how you see yourself, who you believe you are whether good or bad. It is emotion based because it is how you feel about yourself isn't it? If a person has a poor self image it is because they feel a certain way about themselves. It is how the person sees who they believe they are. It is an image that can be changed. There was once a commercial on TV with a blob of paint. A pair of hands changed the picture as the hands rearranged the blob of paint from one image into another. As the commercial went on the image was changed again and again.

What a great picture of God changing our self image. He is constantly transforming us into who He sees and wants us to be. When God comes to transform some of us we tell Him no. We are not willing to let Him transform us. We believe we deserve and will always be the image we presently are. We believe that this is who we are supposed to be, and this is who everyone says we are so that is who we have to be. You do not have to be who people say you are. You can be who God says you are.

When people speak into your life, your emotions respond by convincing you to believe what has been said about you or to reject it. You may believe, "I'm wonderful!" or you may feel you are not loved. You may believe you are smart, will be overweight forever, are too tall, too short, just right, blessed, or even a victim. All of these beliefs are too often based on the emotional response to what others have said or done. Beliefs about who you are usually are based on your emotions rather than on truth. You can change those feelings by aligning yourself with God and agreeing with who He says you are.

This change in your self image may take a little work. Some of this has been sown deeply into you as you have kept going back to it and nurtured these feelings. But God says He is willing to set you free no matter how deeply the seeds of a poor view have personally been sown. He can remove those seeds from the depths of our hearts and transform you with the seeds of who He knows you can become.

In Ezekiel 36:26-29 God said: "I will give you a new heart and put a new spirit in you; I will remove from you your heart of stone and give you a heart of flesh. And I will put my Spirit in you and move you to follow my decrees and be careful to keep my laws. . . . You will be my people, and I will be your God." NIV

In people today the heart of stone may represent a poor self image because in rejecting who God created them to be, they have rejected God's plan and purpose for their lives. Their self image is tied to who people believe they are and it is based on their emotional response to what others have said and done, or are saying and doing to them. This view of who they are is emotionally bound up in their personal experiences. It has everything to do with their emotions overriding God's truth.

There is one of two ways a person chooses their self image; by listening to death words or by trusting God over their emotions. They have either listened to what others have said and have believed the emotional response they have felt toward those words, or they have trusted God and allowed Him to transform them.

I want to be like Jesus and to be like Jesus I have found that trusting God is the better way to go. When looking in Mark 6 you will find that Jesus knew who He was. He did not allow His emotions to color how He viewed Himself even when people said or did things that could have caused a poor self image. Yet He never let that happen. So to be like Jesus means that your self image has to be aligned with who God says you are.

In the first few verses of Mark 6 we find Jesus went back to His home town with His disciples. He usually had people with Him when He was ministering so being like Jesus should most of the time include having people with you when you are ministering. On the Sabbath Jesus was teaching in the Synagogue because He knew who He was and what He was to be doing to advance His Father's Kingdom. The people of his home town began to ask six questions.

1. Where did this man get these things?
2. What is this wisdom given to Him?
3. How are such miracles as these performed by His hands?
4. Isn't this the carpenter?

5. Don't we know His mother, brothers and sisters?
6. Then they were wondering, "Isn't He just a normal guy?"

Wherever a person grows up, most of the time when they go back to their home town there is a familial spirit there that stirs up the old memories. If you have ever been to a reunion the memories of the past begin to be stirred up. Someone may be remembered as the class bully, as the comedian in the family or as the one who was most likely to be successful with their life.

Now picture Jesus in his hometown. He had never sinned? Do you wonder what the people back home were thinking? Do you think they liked Jesus as a child? He always did everything right. If you have known any one that came across that way – always doing everything right, you know they were not always appreciated and generally those around them were looking for that person to make a mistake. For when they made a mistake those around them felt better about themselves. Then they could say, "They are like us!"

Jesus never did make the mistakes; He never did sin. When He showed up in town there were mixed feelings of pride to have one of their own back, and cynicism because He was too perfect. He started teaching with such authority that people were being healed; miracles were taking place right in front of their eyes. Yet, the people of His own town did not want to accept what God was doing through Jesus. So they attempted to change the focus. You can almost hear their discussion.

"Oh, He is just a carpenter. That's all he is, just a carpenter. As a matter of fact, we know His mother Mary. Do you remember His beginnings? Yeah, yeah . . . His parents weren't even married when He was conceived. You know what that makes Him?"

These people who Jesus grew up around started asking these questions and talking this way about Him. They continued, "Weren't his brothers the guys we still know? There are His sisters now. He's no different than we are." And at the end of verse 3 it says "They took offense at Him."

Taking offense is an emotional reaction to somebody. It is a choice every one of us has made depending on the mood we were in at the time. You may have laughed about what one person said, but when another shared similar thoughts you chose to be offended. The difference is your choice to take offense or your choice not to take offense.

Watch the people who are on the news as protestors. They choose to be angry people who have taken offense at something others look at and wonder what the big deal was. Someone once said, "It was a lane change, get over it." But when you take offense, it is difficult to get over it. The offense is fed emotionally so that it grows, bringing a greater emotional response.

In verse 4 Jesus said, "Only in his hometown, among his relatives and in his own house is a prophet without honor." (NIV) He was not able to do many miracles there except lay His hands on a few sick people to heal them. He was amazed at their lack of faith.

Did the Bible say, "Then He went and He pouted because they wouldn't listen to Him and He decided never again to try to do a miracle because He couldn't do many in their presence? He could not believe any longer who God called Him to be. After all they had said He was just a carpenter?!" No, Jesus knew who He was.

Do you want to be like Jesus? Jesus kept doing what God told Him to do. Even when people tried to box Him in to their image of Him by saying, "He's just a carpenter. He's just the brother of James and John . . . and we know them."

Jesus chose to keep doing what Father God was telling Him to do. In this account the reason they did not have many miracles is they were the ones who lacked the faith. Jesus did not lack any faith. Most of the time it is not the person being prayed for that needs the faith. It is the person laying hands on them or declaring healing that needs the faith. But in this case they shut down the miraculous. They chose not to receive what Jesus had for them because their emotional response to Jesus was, "He thinks He is better than we are." Jesus did not say that. He said, "There's a better way for you!"

Jesus stayed focused on His relationship with Father God and who He knew He was. He never lost that focus. When our self image starts to go down and we become more convinced that we are of no value, it is because we have taken our eyes off of our relationship with God, who God has said we are and who He has created us to be. Instead of staying focused and saying, "God this is who You say I am," we slide in one direction or another off the narrow path God has chosen for us to believe the lies that others have spoken. The death words that people have spoken over us seep into our hearts and minds. To truly be like Jesus we have to stay focused on whom Father God has said we are and sees us becoming.

Jesus chose to respond in faith even when they were offended by Him and said all manner of evil against Him; He chose to respond by being there to see people healed. He chose to give out the good news of the Kingdom to a people who did not appear interested because they had chosen an emotional response to be offended by Him.

The passage goes on to tell us that this did not even slow Jesus down. He continued on going from village to village teaching. He called out the twelve giving them authority to heal people and drive out demons. That is not the response of a man who has a poor self image, has lost his focus, or has taken offense at the cruel and hurtful remarks of others made to impact who He was or the calling He was living by.

Some people would listen, some people were not going to listen, but He was going to keep doing what Father God had for Him to do. You are no different. God has created you for His Kingdom work, to advance it in incredible ways. The only factor keeping this from happening in your life is your unwillingness to keep focused on what He has called you to do and be: who He says you are.

He says that you are a minister of the Kingdom of God no matter where you go or what you do. There are people today who recognize that at their place of work they are called by God to minister for His Kingdom. There are believers in places of government who meet to pray and dedicate their work place in the name of Jesus. They can do that because they know who they are in Jesus and they have decided that no matter where they go they are going to live out His calling on their lives. They are going to be who God called them to be.

You are no different. If you are saying, "I'm not licensed, I'm not ordained, I didn't go to Bible School" – thank God that He has chosen you to advance His Kingdom anyway. Who you are and where you are, is exactly where God has placed you for now. You need to figure out what He has for you to do there. If He is saying it is time for a change, it is time for a change because He is about to move you into His purpose for His Kingdom. You may have thought it was so you could receive more money and take better care of your family. Those reasons are further down on the list. At the top of His list is advancing His Kingdom through you. You have to get that in your mindset. You have been chosen by God. You are of great value to His Kingdom. He wants to use you to bring change to a world that desperately needs help.

Why is it that when life gets busy, the first thing so many believers do is step back from ministry and what God has for them because they are too busy now. Why don't believers step back from other activities that have crowded their life out from advancing God's Kingdom? Too often it is because their self worth is tied up in the other activities.

Imagine two little brothers in a discussion at home. If one of them gets mad at the other, does the other get mad as well? Usually he does. This develops into an argument. As they grow up with this manner of dealing with each other, they learn that when someone gets mad at them, they are to get mad right back. Instead of learning to love and honor other people as Romans 12:10 calls them to do, offense is most often taken.

Jesus did not take offense even when others were offended by Him. He kept doing what Father God wanted Him to do. He was God's own Son, isn't there an example of somebody else we could use that was more human? Jesus was just as human as anybody else. He was totally human. Jesus does not take offense today when people take offense at Him. We want to look back at different people in the Bible and say, "What about this person, they made mistakes. What about King David – he was involved in an adulterous affair, he had the husband murdered . . . what about him?"

If David were able to talk with you today, he would not want you to remember him for those actions he took. He would want you to remember that he was a worship leader who loved God, who did the things God wanted him to do and he would not be happy about those things he did that were not what God wanted him to do. He was not known as a man after God's own heart because of the wrong he did.

Yet people often want to step back into those comfort zones where others are kind of messed up. So that they can say it's okay to be messed up. The only person we should want to be like is Jesus Christ, nobody else. It does not matter what else took place in some one else's life. What matters the most is for each of us to keep our eyes on Jesus Christ, then you can help other people. If you are trying to compare yourself to others, you will become distracted and will lower your self image at the same time. You lower your self image because the Bible says you are made in the image of God, not in the image of someone who is not God.

Do not use this as an excuse to judge someone because they are not doing what you think they should be doing or saying. If you keep your focus on Jesus by loving them and honoring them, your self image will improve. Do you know why there are so many problems in the Church today? Why there are so many denominations and believers who will not talk to each other or will not affiliate with each other? We do not love and honor each other. It is that simple. If you love and honor somebody then you will continue to minister with them. Yet if you do not love and honor them, you will find ways to pick at them and what they are doing, resulting in your withdrawal from one of God's family members. Most of the time people pick at others and find out what is wrong with them is because their own self image wants to raise them up to the other person's level, or to pull the other person down to their level. That is a self image based on emotions which have run amok.

Jesus did not do that. He knew who He was, He believed who He was, and He acted on who He was. You and I have to know who we are, we have to believe who we are, and we have to act on who we are in Jesus Christ. If you take nothing else away from this chapter – know that you must learn who you are in Jesus Christ, believe who you are in Jesus Christ, and act on it.

Here is some helpful counsel.

1.  God loves you. Accept this truth and look for His love each day. If you are having a hard time believing God loves you – that is a self image issue. The Bible is full of the truth that God loves you. Your life is also full of examples of how much He loves you. Bask in His love. Tell God, "You love me God." Tell

other people, "God loves me." Learn to accept His love from others when they extend it to you.

When people first fall in love they bask in the other person's love. They receive letters; they read the letters, not just once but multiple times. Read your Bible.

2. Learn to recognize what God does for you as acts of His love. It is not about what you get from God but about His love for you.

3. Read the following truths out loud everyday until they have been endeared to your heart. Someone sent this to me, I am not sure who put all these truths together in this way, but this is a great tool for improving our self image.

I KNOW WHO I AM - I am God's child (John 1:12). I am Christ's friend (John 15:15). I am united with the Lord (1 Cor. 6:17). I am bought with a price (1 Cor. 6:19-20). I am a saint (set apart for God). (Eph. 1:1). I am a personal witness of Christ (Acts 1:8). I am the salt & light of the earth (Matt. 5:13-14). I am a member of the body of Christ (1 Cor 12:27). I am free forever from condemnation (Rom. 8: 1-2). I am a citizen of Heaven. I am significant (Phil.3:20). I am free from any charge against me (Rom. 8:31-34). I am a minister of reconciliation for God (2 Cor.5:17-21). I have access to God through Holy Spirit (Eph 2:18). I am seated with Christ in the heavenly realms (Eph. 2:6). I cannot be separated from the love of God (Rom.8:35-39). I am established, anointed, sealed by God (2 Cor.1:21-22). I am assured all things work together for good (Rom. 8: 28). I have been chosen and appointed to bear fruit (John 15:16). I may approach God with freedom and confidence (Eph. 3: 12). I can do all things in Christ who strengthens me (Phil. 4:13). I am the branch of the true vine, a channel of His life (John 15: 1-5). I am God's temple (1 Cor. 3: 16). I am complete in Christ (Col. 2: 10). I am hidden with Christ in God (Col. 3:3). I have been justified (Romans 5:1). I am God's co-worker (1 Cor. 3:9; 2 Cor 6:1). I am God's workmanship (Eph. 2:10). I am confident that the good works God has begun in me will be perfected (Phil. 1: 5). I have been redeemed and forgiven (Col. 1:14). I have been adopted as God's child (Eph 1:5). I belong to God.

We have to know and believe who we are in Jesus Christ to have our self image changed. If you do not believe these things are true about you then you must realize you are caught in the Poor Self Image syndrome. What else can a person do to break free of a poor self image?

1.  Tell God what the emotional struggles are in your life. Be honest with God and admit to Him where you need help. You may need to tell Him, "God I really struggle with this person at work and this is why." It is important to figure out why you struggle with a person so you can overcome that issue by turning it into a prayer of blessing in their life. If you struggle with a person because whenever you are around them they are critical; the Lord would have you pray blessings into their life so you are able to be a person who blesses others, not be a critic. Pray something like, "Lord bless them with a positive outlook on life. Bless them with wonderful things so they see the good in everything." When we bless people it affects our emotional response to them.

2.  Change the way you believe by no longer agreeing with the wrong thoughts. When those thoughts come, God's Spirit will begin to move and instead of saying, "He's doing it again," you change the way you believe by saying, "Lord he's doing that again because you want to change him by demonstrating your love to him. So I bless them with a move of your

Spirit in his life. Lord, since I see it and it bothers me so much, you need to change me, too. Please change me so that when I see that person I see good things. I see who you see that person is, for who they are." As God changes you, then everything else is changed as your perspective changes. Our self image is tied, not just ourselves, but to how we see others.

3. Renounce the wrong emotions that you struggle with. Speak to anger in your life and tell it you no longer want anything to do with it. Tell judgmentalism you do not want anything to do with it anymore. Doubt, fear, shame, jealousy – any emotion that has kept you from being like Jesus. If you have done this before and these emotions keep coming, you need to keep doing it. The more you renounce these things, the less of a hold they will have on you.

4. Agree with God. Trust Him by doing what he wants. The way to overcome doubt is to believe by moving in faith. Tell God you agree with Him that He wants you to move in love, to honor everybody above yourself. Agree this is how you are supposed to treat everybody else and begin treating them in these ways. If you start treating others in these ways out of a changed heart and mindset then these actions will effectively help you see yourself differently. We are radically transformed when we do what God wants us to do. When we love and honor someone else, our change in what we believe brings a change in who we are. In marriage counseling the best advice that can be given is for the husband to be the best husband he can be. For the wife to be the best wife she can be. This choice will transform their marriage. As that changes the person, their spouse will see and this will have an incredible impact on them. God is

always more interested in changing me for His glory than I am in being changed.

A lady in our congregation shared these thoughts with me. "As I was driving home I heard, 'the operative word in breakthrough is break. You have to break the old to bring forth the new'. I had a picture of soil breaking open to allow a delicate seed to sprout. At first the soil was very hard and cracked. As the healing rains came the cracks filled with water to allow the soil to soften once again. When the soil is soft and ready, new growth will occur. God is breaking us up so we can become new creatures in Him. Breaking strongholds, destructive habit patterns and thought processes, old defense mechanisms. The old way that we see ourselves, God is breaking that up too. We have to want to receive; we cannot let the hard condition of our hearts to allow the healing waters to pass us by. Instead we need to allow the water to penetrate the cracks until the soil becomes soft and ready to be broken up and prepared for planting something new within us. For some the soil is too hard and the water will roll right over the top rather than sinking in. We need help from a gardener who knows what tools to use to break up the soil. Will we allow Him to use His tools to help loosen us up or allow the thorny weeds, which are the only things that can grow in that kind of soil, to keep our hearts hard? Hard hearts keep us from becoming who we are meant to be."

If you struggle with a poor self image, it is not what God intends you to believe about yourself. He did not create you that way. You have allowed what other people have said, other actions that have been taken against you, or by you to cause you to begin to believe the things that are not true about you. The most important thing you can do today is receive God's love. Let God love you.

If you are not sure you know how to receive God's love, you could start by just waiting on Him. Find a place to be alone with God and while worshipping Him allow His incredible love to move within you. If you sing the songs but not the words, by singing something you do not mean with your heart, then you will miss His love.

Perhaps you have been at a birthday party where the person whose life is being celebrated has ripped through the gifts. When the gift opening time is over people have wondered if the person even appreciated what had been given to them. Have you ever wondered if God feels that way? He has given us such incredible gifts which we often do not recognize He has given to us. He loves us so much.

Think about the verse that says, "For God *so loved* the world that *He gave His only Son*, that whoever believes in Him *will not perish but have* everlasting life." That should be a verse that impacts our lives when we hear it, when we quote it. Read it over again slowly – "For God *so loved the world* that *He gave His only Son*, that *whoever* believes in Him *will not perish but* have everlasting life."

If you have yet to give your life to Jesus Christ, surrender your life by committing yourself to following Him – for this book to have the deepest impact in your life you are hoping for, you need to surrender to Jesus. There is no mystical prayer formula to surrendering your life. You need to have a conversation with God. Tell Him that you want to surrender your life to Him, giving up who you are to be; who He sees you will become. You will need to grow in your understanding of who Jesus Christ is in your life, so it will be good for you to find a local congregation that loves God, enjoys worshiping Him. Develop relationships with people who know God and are willing to help you know God. Being with people who are motivated to know, love and experience God will help you develop the image of God in you in the positive way Father God intended.

If you are taking this first step of accepting God's power to change your life today, congratulations! He will never leave you, never forsake you and He is already present in your life. You just have to get to know Him to recognize how good He is and how much He loves you.

# Chapter 4

# The "How Does That Make You Feel?" Syndrome

The story is told of a grandma who was putting on her makeup in the bathroom under the watchful eye of her young granddaughter as she had done many times before. After she applied her lipstick and started to leave the little one said: "But Grandma, you forgot to kiss the toilet paper goodbye."

A young grandson called one day to wish his grandfather a happy birthday. When he asked his grandfather how old he was the boy was told sixty two. It was quiet for a moment and then the little one said, "Did you start at one?"

After putting her grandchildren to bed a grandmother changed into old slacks and a droopy blouse in order to wash her hair. When she heard the children getting more and more rambunctious her patience grew very thin. Finally she threw a towel around her head stormed into their room putting them back to bed with stern warnings and as she left the room she heard the three year old ask, "Who was that?"

How do you think they felt when they heard these responses? Most of the time we do not think about why we feel a certain way. We put such an emphasis on our emotions that often we just ask, "How does that make you feel?" How many times have you heard that question?

We have been taught that how we feel is of way too high of importance to us and others in many areas of our society for several decades. The question, "How does that make you feel?" implies that whatever a person is feeling, whatever the emotional state that they are in, should be validated as legitimate simply because it is an emotion they are experiencing. We have been taught that however you feel, whatever your emotions are telling you is legitimate.

The simple phrase, "How does that make you feel?" has elevated the importance of people's emotions above logic, above spiritual truth, and even at times above God's Holy Spirit. Emotions are a temporary state of your heart while God's word is an eternal. What God's Spirit says to you needs to have greater significance in your life than your emotions ever do. Your emotions need to be weighed in light of God's truth, not the other way around. Rather than looking at the Bible and saying how does that make you feel, you should look at your emotions and ask what God's Word says about what has happened? What does God want you to do in that moment rather than how you feel about what is happening?

We hear statements like: "I feel so in love with him." What one does with that feeling demonstrates if their feelings have greater influence in their lives than God's written Word. That feeling often leads people to think it is alright to have sex with the person they have this feeling toward, outside of a marriage commitment. God's Word says it is never alright to have sex outside of marriage. Many believers have chosen to go after this type of feeling rather than follow through on what God wants for their lives. When they choose how they feel over obeying God they will always find themselves in trouble.

While talking with some believers in Jesus Christ after a prayer meeting, one of them started getting worked up about a couple of social issues and in particular abortion. I was able to share that God has said "if My people, who are called by name will humble themselves and pray, and turn from their wicked ways . . . I will heal the land." He did not say "if the people who do not know Me will turn from their ways." God said if "My people" will turn from "their" ways.

We talked about abortion being a symptom of a different issue. The issue in most cases is that people become pregnant because they have had sex outside of marriage. They chose what felt good, rather than choosing action that is good: obeying God. They found themselves in trouble and chose again not to obey God.

If the Church would understand that God says sex outside of marriage is wrong, God says do not do it, and if the Church believed this truth to the point of living it out, there would be fewer abortions because God's people would stop having sex outside of their marriage relationship.

A couple of years ago I was privileged to preside over eight weddings in a period of eleven months. Of the eight marriages, only two of the eight couples had not slept together before getting married. Every one of the people getting married had told me they were Christians. The Church is rife with this issue, and it is a spiritual issue. This is happening because we have bought into the mindset that says "if you feel like doing it, it is okay."

We have come to the place where we listen to and follow our emotions over the word of God. Whether it is sex, anger, or most issues of our heart. Emotions began to take hold in society years ago. Their importance has carried so much into the church that emotions are too highly esteemed even there – both in individual lives as well as corporately. Congregations take surveys and polls of their people to see how they feel about what is happening, instead of asking God what He wants them to do in order to lead His people in His ways.

This demonstrates how people have bought into the philosophy of relativism. Relativism is the belief that there is no truth. Every decision made is determined by people's emotional response based on the circumstances or situation people find themselves in at the time. Relativism teaches that no matter what situation a person comes into there is no right or wrong way to act. Each person can do whatever they feel like doing. There is no standard by which people should live their lives. God's Word says that is not true, but relativism links with our emotions to say, "I can do whatever I want in any situation. As long as it does not hurt anybody else, then it is okay." The problem is that every decision we make affects somebody else in some way. Accepting this mindset and living it out demonstrates that people have placed their emotions as the highest level of authority in their lives, even above God.

From the time they are infants; most people are taught that their emotions are of highest importance in their lives. Think about it. This is why everyone is encouraged to express how they feel and believe their feelings should be important. When a Board is meeting and looking for consensus they may ask the members present, "how does that make you feel?" Or perhaps they may say, "Before we go on do you feel good about that decision?"

When people are asked what they think, their responses often reflect one of these answers. "Well, I'm feeling like maybe I should . . . ." instead of, "the truth of the matter is . . . ." When on a jury the judge gives specific instructions to the jury, which they are only to consider during the time of deliberation. They are to base their decision on those specific instructions. The instructions are given to help the jurors come to a legal rationale by which they are able to declare the defendant guilty or not guilty. The decision by the jury is not supposed to be determined by how the jurors feel about the defendant, the judge, the prosecuting attorney, or the facts but it is to be based solely on the evidence presented.

In a case in which I was privileged to be on a jury, one of the instructions the judge told us to use in making our determination was, "did this person knowingly commit the crime." The defendant had testified during the case that he had known that selling the drugs was a crime. As the Jury Foreman began going around the room asking people for their decisions based on the instructions of the judge, some of the jury members began sharing their feelings about the case. "You know, it didn't seem fair because . . ." was a phrase being used. The third person said, "According to the instructions of the judge, it doesn't matter what we feel is fair, all that matters is the defendant said, he knew what he was doing. He knew it was a crime. He did it anyway." The jurors may have felt bad for the defendant and still have done what was right. Or they may have decided to base their decision on the emotional context. When people base their decisions on the emotional context of a situation, they will often make an unjust decision. Basing one's decision on the truth of a matter does not always make people feel good.

Some wonder if there is a difference between "I'm feeling like we should do this" and "the truth of the matter is . . . ." They ask "isn't one just a nicer way of saying something?" Not always; more often than not people are finding a way to express an emotional response rather than the truth of what should take place. The Church has to get past this in order to live in the truth.

People who do not know Jesus Christ can be expected to act like they do not know Jesus Christ because they do not know Him. But people who know Jesus Christ need to do what Jesus would do and need to be incredible examples of who Jesus is. When we get to heaven it will not wash if God asks a person why they made a certain decision and the response is, "You know I was just feeling like maybe that would be a good thing."

When someone stands before God at the end of their life, if God asks why He should let them into His heaven, and they respond, "I feel like I was a pretty good person," they will not have given the right answer. If they respond, "There were times I just didn't feel what You wanted me to do was very loving so I decided to do what I felt like," that will not cut it either. The Bible says there is one reason we will be allowed into heaven and it will be based on our having given our lives to Jesus Christ and made Him our Lord and Savior.

During a City Council meeting one of the Council members displayed his emotions about a recommendation by one of the subcommittees being questioned after it had been through discussions by the committee as a whole. When he became upset during the City Council meeting and began voicing his emotional irritation at the change being proposed, one of the other Council members was going to vote for the recommendation but changed his vote. Because the first Council member acted the way he did, the second council member deliberately changed his vote.

If a decision has been made because it is the right decision for the city and a Council member reacts emotionally about the issue, is the decision no longer the right thing to do? Is it still the right thing to do? If a person's emotions determine that they are going to teach another person a lesson by changing their vote, is that not allowing their emotions to over-rule what is right? Why would that be acceptable to people? Why would people step back and think that changing one's vote was the right decision because the other person had acted poorly? If the decision was the right decision, it was the right decision whether the other person responded emotionally or not.

We have to understand our emotions and the correct role they are to have in our lives. Rather than ask "how does that make you feel?" the better question is, "why do you feel that way?"

Think about how the following questions and statements make you feel.

1.  How do you feel when you hear someone say "I saw someone hit a dog the other day"? (Now let me add this to the statement. A couple was walking their small dog when a pit bulldog broke through a fence, attacked the smaller dog and the owner of the small dog hit the pit bulldog. Do you feel differently now about what you were asked?)
2.  How do you feel about the statement, "They look so cute together?"
3.  How do you feel when you are at a Worship Gathering or a theater watching a movie and someone is clipping their fingernails?
4.  If you hear "Your rights are being stepped on by another person and you shouldn't have to take that," what are you feeling?
5.  How do you feel if someone says, "No matter what you do, God loves you. No matter what you've done, God still loves you?"
6.  How do you feel if you hear, "God may love you but Satan wants to destroy you?" Did that put fear in your heart, or did you realize it does not matter because God loves you and will protect you?

Everything that is said to us somehow stirs up some kind of an emotion. There are always at least two ways to respond in any given situation.

In 1 Samuel 30 David had been living among the Philistines while going out and raiding other places. After each raid, he and his men had been returning to Ziklag. The time came for the Philistines to go out to war with Israel and David and his men were called on to go with them. But when they arrived the Rulers of the Philistines decided they could not trust David and his men because the Philistines were going to war with the nation David had led in many victorious battles. The rulers decided to send them back to Ziklag.

When they arrived at Ziklag at the beginning of 1 Samuel 30, they found the Amalekites had raided Ziklag having taken captive all of the women and children, as well as everything David and his warriors owned. Think of what that would be like. How would that make you feel?

When these six hundred warriors found that Ziklag had been destroyed by fire and their wives, children and possessions had all been taken they wept out loud until they had no strength left to weep. Now that was an emotional response. I think it was the right one. It is necessary and good to grieve at times.

David, who had lost both his wives, was terribly upset. Not just because of his family being gone, but the men were talking about killing him. The men were bitter because they had lost their families and possessions yet David found his strength in God. Here were two different responses based on emotions. The men wanted to kill David because they were looking for someone to blame while David wanted God to make Him strong to lead.

We see that all the time today. No matter what has happened, a crisis in our city or town – people are always looking for someone to put the blame on. They want to put the hurt on them because somehow that makes people feel better emotionally if they think it was somebody else's fault. It is why when Hurricane Katrina hit New Orleans; people found a way to say it was the government's fault.

The warriors who were committed to following David were coming after their leader. He was anointed by God to be the king and they wanted to stone him to death because somebody else came and stole their women and children.

Does that make any sense at this moment? When these men were in this emotional state of mind it made all kinds of sense. When our emotional reaction is to look for who is to blame, our perception will distort the reality of the moment. Often mistakes are made when we emotionally react in a situation.

David did not get caught up in their reaction, but found strength in the Lord his God. He called for the priest to bring the ephod so David could discern what God wanted him to do. God told David to pursue the Amalekites. God said David would overtake them and succeed in the rescue. With six hundred men ready to stone him to death, David's emotional reaction could have been to jump on a horse and get away. Instead, David turned to God. David chose to find his strength in God by asking God what to do. Do you see the difference in the two responses?

David and the six hundred men took off and on the way two hundred became so exhausted physically that they could not continue the pursuit. These men had marched for three days to get home, they had wept until they had no strength left, and then they march off again to catch up with the people who have taken their wives, children and possessions. David had the exhausted men wait where they were and the other four hundred went with David to rescue their families. When they came back to the two hundred who were waiting the evil men and trouble makers among the four hundred did not want to give the two hundred an equal share in the plunder David brought back.

This was another emotional reaction by a group of David's warriors. What was it based on? It was based on selfishness, self centeredness and greed. David responded by telling the men that they were not to do that with what the Lord had given to them. All the plunder they had collected and brought back was from God according to David and therefore they were going to have to split it up with everybody. Not only that but David sent some of the plunder to the leaders of Judah telling them that it was a portion of the spoils from the Lord's enemies for them.

David recognized that God had given them so much they needed to give some of it away to people who had needs. The evil rebellious ones had responded emotionally with greed and selfish desires while David had responded emotionally in a completely different manner. David had to stand before these men and tell them they were wrong and he was not going to let them get away with it.

Emotions that are a response to what God wants will demonstrate the image of God in us accurately to a world that desperately needs to see how emotions can be controlled instead of allowing emotions to control them. But they can distort our perception of reality and we can use our emotions to make it sound like anything is the right thing to do. Those men thought they were responding logically because they went out and risked their lives so they felt they should have gotten the plunder. But it was not what God wanted.

In every situation of our lives we have at least two responses. We can respond with our emotions based on what we think is right or we can go to God and ask what He wants us to do in the situation, how He wants us to respond, and what He wants us to say? In following God in this way our godly emotional response shows others how God wants people to use their emotions.

All of those who stayed behind saw in David the love of God. They witnessed and experienced the mercy and the grace of God. Every time you make a decision to help others when someone else says, "I don't want to help," God's mercy and grace are seen through you. God demonstrates his mercy and grace to us every day. God never says you have used up your share of His mercy and grace no matter how long the week seems to have been. While God never does that, sometimes it seems like we might do that to people.

In our society, "how does that make you feel?" has morphed into, "everyone's emotions are legitimate." People are too concerned today about anyone being offended. Someone may say, "I'm feeling like if we say someone's personal views are wrong it might hurt their feelings. So we should be careful to acknowledge their feelings." However a person feels is a legitimate thing in the society we live. It has caused a deescalating stairwell. This means that we as a people are going to keep circling down until we reach the point where people are willing to allow whatever wrong thoughts and feelings someone has to be acknowledged as correct. It will be as though how they feel in the moment is right.

If you want to be like Jesus, being offended is never the correct emotional response to what somebody has done to you. Jesus was never offended by what was done to Him. If you are wondering about the time at the temple when He took the cords and made them into a whip; He drove the people out who were selling overpriced livestock to people at the temple in order for them to have "clean" animals to sacrifice. Think about it. He did not respond that way because of what they were doing to Him personally. It was because of what they were doing to the temple, the house of His Father.

Jesus who always did what Father God wanted offended the religious leaders of His time. Jesus took the time to explain to the religious leaders why following tradition instead of following the commands of God was wrong in Matthew 15. They had grown to love their traditions more than loving God. If it was tradition, they were not to think about it, just do it. Jesus pointed out that they were nullifying the Word of God for the sake of their tradition. They honored tradition above even the Scriptures. Tradition was how they lived; it was how they had been taught to live. Tradition had gone beyond what God had said to do and was someone's interpretation of what God meant.

Jesus told them they were taking the Word of God and ignoring it, nullifying it by fulfilling their traditions over God's Word. He went on to call them hypocrites to their face. The word hypocrite referred to Greek actors. The actors would take a mask, put it over their face and pretend to be someone they were not. They were acting a part and the mask they thought helped them play the role better. Jesus was telling the Religious Leaders that they were hypocrites, hiding who they were behind a mask of false spirituality. Everything they felt would be wonderful if they followed what tradition dictated.

The entire discussion came out of an accusation by the religious leaders against Jesus' disciples because they were not washing their hands. He told them that they honored God with their lips but their hearts were far from God. They said things about God that their hearts were not living out. He pointed out that their worship of God was in vain, in an empty way. He explained to them that their teachings were rules from men, not from God as they claimed. For they had taken the Old Testament Law and in attempting to under-stand how to live what God meant, they added to the law their own teaching of dos and don'ts. You could only walk so far on the Sabbath if you were going to keep it holy for example. If someone was sick they were not to be healed on the Sabbath. Yet if their animal had fallen in a pit, they would work to get their animal out on the Sabbath.

Before we become judgmental, the Church has done similar things. There is a tendency in trying to please God to establish rules and requirements the Bible does not. It starts out as thinking of ways to please God, but turns into tradi-tions. There are times the Church has explained what the

Bible has said based on their understanding and left people with the impression that this understanding was the only way God could possibly have meant what the Bible said.

Some are taught that there are no longer apostles and prophets. Even though the Bible says there will be apostles and prophets until we all have attained the unity of the faith and know the Son of God (Eph 4:13), their tradition has taught them to believe something different than what the Bible teaches. So they reject anyone or any teaching that says there are apostles and prophets.

Some have been taught that only those who are members of their local congregation are able to partake in communion. So unless a person has joined that congregation or denomination, even if they love Jesus, are not allowed to partake in communion with those believers. That is a tradition; it is not what Jesus taught.

Some believe that if there is not an organ playing then you are not able to truly worship. Some believe that if there is not a guitar playing then you are not able to worship. There are those who refuse to use any kind of musical instrument when they worship. Some believe you have to kneel a certain number of times for it to be worship. Others believe you have to sing hymns to worship. Then there are those who believe you should worship in whatever way makes you feel good. When something does not fit into what we have been taught we reject it as wrong and we find ourselves in a similar position as the religious leaders of Jesus' day. Certain of what we feel or have been taught is correct, uncertain if what someone else is doing is right.

It was Isaiah who originally shared the prophetic word that Jesus taught in Matthew 15:8. Thousands of years ago the prophet told people that their traditions had become more valuable to them than what the Word of God said. In our desire to please God sometimes we have fallen into the same activity. Traditions are not necessarily wrong unless they are elevated above the Word of God.

Jesus then turned to the people to explain that ceremonially washing one's hands was not what made them clean. What went into a person's mouth was not what defiled a person; it was what came out of their mouth that defiled them. Washing one's hands was not part of God's law. It was a tradition that had been established by the religious leaders. Probably every elementary school child today would rise up and cheer if they knew Jesus said this because they do not always want to wash their hands. While we wash our hands today as a part of personal hygiene, Jesus' "new" teaching ran contrary to the traditions of the religious leaders.

This new teaching bothered the religious leaders so much that the disciples came to Jesus to ask Him if He knew that these religious leaders were offended when they heard this statement. Do you wonder how the disciples knew they were offended? Do you think they walked up to the religious leaders and asked, "How does that make you feel when Jesus said that? Are you okay with that?"

Have we ever done that in the Church? God is doing something and we walk over to someone and say, "Are you okay with what is going on? How does this make you feel?" instead of pointing out that God is at work in that moment.

The disciples were quick to tell Jesus that He had offended the Religious Leaders. Did Jesus say, "You know, you are right, I should not have said that to them. Call them all back here. I'll tell them I may have overstated what I was saying and I will apologize." No, He did not.

Instead He said, "Every plant which My heavenly Father did not plant shall be uprooted. Let them alone; they are blind guides of the blind. And if a blind man guides a blind man, both will fall into a pit."

Today if someone asks another person if they know they have offended someone else it seems that everyone feels that the person speaking what appears to be offending words needs to go back and apologize to make sure the other person feels better. Even to the point that people can lose their job for something they have said, because someone took offense at it.

Jesus does not seem to be nearly as concerned about people's feelings and emotions as He is about truth being spoken in love. Let's make clear a couple of issues that some may be wondering about.

The first is whether we should care about offending people. We should be more concerned about speaking the truth in love than whether someone is taking offense. Since Romans 12:18 says: "If possible, so far as it depends on you, be at peace with all men." We should watch what we say because often it is not what is said but the tone in which we communicate that offends. On any given day your spouse or child may come into the house making a statement that you laugh at. The next day they could come in and say the exact same thing but their tone of voice or the mood you are in now causes you to take offense. We need to be careful of how we speak as Ephesians 4:15 tells us to speak the truth in love. Yet even when the truth has been spoken in love there are times when people have still taken offense.

Secondly, please notice that it is the individual's choice to be offended by something. Each of us is personally responsible for taking offense. Being offended is an emotional choice. Whether someone is offended by what may have been said or done. Why is it that sometimes we walk away from a conversation without being offended, and at other times the words bring us to a place that we choose to be offended? It all depends on our emotional response. This is why talk radio plays on people's emotions. The talk radio host knows if they can get an emotional response out of people their ratings will improve.

Bear in mind that if someone chooses to be offended, it could end your relationship. This may make it necessary for one to go back to the person who has taken offense to be sure they understood the truth you were attempting to bring forth. If it was the truth that offended them, you need to speak the truth anyway as long as you have done it in love and in an attempt to help the other person understand. Too often today what people speak is neither truth nor have they spoken it in love. Rather than the truth we often share our perception of the truth.

Our leaders were presented with two issues a few years back that involved following through on what Jesus taught in Matthew 18 about restoring relationships. A concern at the time was would we offend the person we were going to privately approach when we took the second step of speaking to the one who had sinned against another and had not been willing to repent. The issue in this type of life situation is not whether they are offended but whether the ones approaching them are able to win them back in love. It is possible that anyone who has chosen not to change their mind when confronted with a sin in their lives is going to be offended when approached. Yet Jesus said it is the right thing to do.

People may choose to be offended at the truth when the issue is their problem. People take offense because of how what is said has made them feel. If we choose to be offended by the way someone says something, it is still our problem. We can hold onto how someone talked to us the rest of our lives, or we can let it go and move on with our lives. Being offended is a choice that we make.

It may surprise you to know there have been congregations where people have been offended by the choice of color in a restroom. Some people are easily offended, are you? For some it is the color of the carpet, the style of the worship music, a restroom that has run out of toilet paper.

While toilet paper is important, don't get me wrong, the lack of its presence in a restroom is not a reason to be offended.

We had a worship team member who was seen outside smoking a cigarette between Worship Services. One of our ladies who took offense at this and came to tell me because she felt they should be kicked off the worship team. My approach was to ask if it was better to let them smoke outside between services or to tell them they were not in a place in life where God was willing to use their talents because they were doing something that one of our members took offense to. God had been using worship to draw this person back to Jesus and their life was in the process of changing. Gratefully this particular lady who was an Elder's wife understood and chose to no longer take offense and in a matter of time God had moved to change some of the habits of the worship team member's life. We chose to love them and let God be responsible for changing their heart and then their actions.

Be careful when you choose to be offended. More often than not, what you choose to be offended by is not something God is offended by. He understands who we are. Psalm 103 says "He remembers how He formed us, that we are dust." He gives us so much more room and so much more grace than we give each other. Rather than be offended at someone the Bible tells us that love covers a multitude of sins. Instead of reacting because they may not have spoken the truth in love, why do we find it so hard to let it go? Why hold on to that, make a grudge out of it and carry it around? Because it did not make us feel good? We are so wounded and in need of healing that we often stockpile offenses one after another. Do you see that Jesus came to redeem us and set us free?

We need to learn to choose joy over our emotions. We can do that because joy is not an emotion, it is an attitude. Joy is one of the fruit of the Spirit. In Philippians 2:17 Paul wrote: "But even if I am being poured out as a drink offering upon the sacrifice and service of your faith, I rejoice and share my joy with you all." Here was a man in jail. He could be offended, he could be upset; he could be crying out, "God why have you put me here?" Instead he had joy. Joy is not an emotion it is a fruit God gives that helps your heart to be right before Him. With joy you can come to a place where in the midst of suffering you will say, "It's alright, I trust God. I have joy in the midst of my circumstances."

Hebrews 2 tells us to fix our eyes on Jesus who chose the joy and endured the cross. I want to be like Jesus. You may not have the emotion of being happy in the midst of the circumstance, yet you can be full of joy. God will give you joy. If your emotions allow other feelings to come up, take those to God. Ask Him if you are supposed to be feeling that way. Ask God to replace the feelings with joy. Philippians 4:4 says to rejoice in the Lord always. Always means not just when you feel like rejoicing. To rejoice means that you had joy so you are able to have joy again. Rather than first choosing our emotional response, we choose God's joy.

God's people should start asking the question, "Why do you feel that way?" instead of, "How does that make you feel?" When with a person who seems down, ask them why they feel the way they do. They need to understand why they feel the way they do so that they can learn to control and deal with their emotions by discovering what God wants them to do with the emotions.

Here are six activities that will help you learn to control your emotions.

1.  Determine you are going to be like Jesus. It does not matter what anyone else wants to do or who they want to be like, determine that you are going to be like Jesus. John Fischer wrote the song "Righteous Man" which says "I'm going to march to a different drum, even if I'm the only one. I want to hear when I'm done, you did well my son." Jesus never chose to

be offended by what others did to Him or said about Him.

2. Ask yourself if there is an example of Jesus and how He responded emotionally. Throughout the gospels Jesus responded to situations and people emotionally because He was human and His emotions were part of the image of God. Look for a situation similar to what you may be going through to understand how Jesus responded.

3. Understand why you chose a different emotion than Jesus did. Stop and evaluate why you chose an emotion that Jesus did not choose. If He is supposed to be sitting on the throne of your life, your emotions may have been overshadowing Him. When you gave your life to Jesus it meant that from that time on He has lived within you so you can respond the way He responded. Remind yourself that "It is no longer I who live but Christ lives in me. The life I know live in the flesh I live by faith in the Son of God who loved me and gave Himself up for me." (Gal 2:20) You can choose Jesus' emotions because He sits on the throne of your life.

4. If your emotions well up so large that you cannot see Jesus and you choose the wrong emotion then after confessing this to God you need to know you are forgiven (1 John 1:9). You will be able to see Jesus again clearly. I am convinced that most people who know this verse do not truly believe it. If we did believe it, when we confessed our sins we would be able to let them go. If you think about it, Jesus still responds with His emotions toward people today.

5. Begin choosing to respond with Jesus' emotions today. This is going to take some time to develop. For many years you have chosen to respond according to how you may have felt. For a habit to be formed one

has to practice it for weeks. So do not allow your-self to become discouraged if you choose the wrong emotion for a while. Just keep going back to Jesus and choosing to be like Him by learning to control your emotions.

6.  Find someone who you know to talk with about your emotions. When you have someone who will help you discover how Jesus responds, change will come quicker. If you are concerned that asking someone to help you will allow them to see that you may have issues, they already know. Calling out to another person for prayer will strengthen you and strengthen them. Figure out who you can call on when you are struggling with your emotions. If you are married, give your spouse room to call on someone besides you. They do not always need to tell you if they are struggling with something. Sometimes it may be better if you do not know because of how you may respond with your emotions.

There have been times I have needed to talk with another man to ask for his prayers. My elders have come to me before to say they were concerned about an emotional response in my life. I was choosing to be disappointed by the way a staff member had been responding to me. I looked at what they were saying and needed to admit to them they were right. We stopped and prayed together for me and by God's power I changed my emotion of disappointment to one of expectation. It was an example of iron sharpening iron. Our emotions are not something we have to fight with by ourselves. We need other people. That is why together we make up the body of Christ.

If my right arm thought it was not going to be my right arm and fell off in the corner would that make it no longer my right arm? It would still be my right arm. My body would be walking around saying, "Man that hurts." We are the body of Christ where all these parts are supposed to be fitting together and some of us think we can lop part of our body off and not have it be a part of the rest of us. We cannot think we are just the pinky of the Church and the Church does not need a pinky. When you cut off your pinky, it still hurts no matter how small you may think it is. So let others help you reconnect to the body so you will experience the love of others. We love our pinky fingers, they do things our thumbs cannot do.

Find people that you are able to talk with about your emotions. Share with them how you reacted and ask them how you could have responded differently. Then pray with them about responding differently. Give them the power to touch your life. Jesus said in John 5:19 "Truly, truly, I say to you, the Son can do nothing of Himself, unless it is something He sees the Father doing; for whatever the Father does, these things the Son also does in like manner." Jesus, who was totally human, always did what Father God did. So when we want to be like Jesus we want to do what God does and Father God controls his emotions.

In John 5:30 Jesus said: "I can do nothing on My own initiative. . . . I do not seek My own will, but the will of Him who sent Me." The key to responding with the correct emotions is to seek to do the will of God. Be like Jesus and do only what Father God has for you to do. As you do this Holy Spirit will make you into a person who emotionally responds according to what Father God wants and no longer according to what your flesh wants. Rather than allow our emotions to take over and run amok, remember that emotions are part of the image of God and therefore were given to you by God.

# Chapter 5

# The "Medicate It" Disorder

God allows pharmaceutical companies and their research to develop medications and He allows doctors to know when to use them. There are people who these medications help. What this chapter shares needs to be kept in the context of that fact. You will not read and should not think that I believe there is never a time to go to a doctor, nor should you believe that God does not use medications to help with healing. But know that while God uses medical knowledge it was not what God intended. Yet people tend to run to medications before they seek the God of the universe for their healing, and that tendency often outweighs our ability to trust God and to have faith in God's power.

Our first reaction most of the time when we have sore muscles is to run to the pain relievers that are plentiful today. I know a chiropractor who likes to say, "Pain is good, it let's you know you are alive". There are times it is okay for our muscles to ache when we have been outside working or we have done some things that are a normal part of life. We have a tendency to run too quickly to medicate ourselves. If we stretched our muscles and were careful how we lifted or carried weight we would have less of a need for pain relievers.

There are many times what we medicate covers up the spiritual condition that has caused the problem. At this point I am not talking about sore muscles but about other issues of our life that we medicate. We know some people who enjoy drinking wine who bring up jokingly that wine is cheaper than Valium. There are people with such emotional lows that they will medicate themselves to stabilize their emotions. They are encouraged to do this to keep themselves on a level plain emotionally to feel okay. These are people who have so emotionally bottomed out that they have found it necessary to look for medical help.

The goal of these kinds of medications is to bring people from a place where their emotions no longer drag their soul and spirit down by leveling out their emotional state. Sometimes the meds make matters worse; sometimes they make them better depending on how quickly the medical professionals are able to find the right amount to give someone who is struggling. Even the correct meds need to be adjusted and they take time to work. They are not a save all for people. The purpose is to deaden one's emotions so some stability can come into the individual's life during the time they are taking them.

One spiritual issue caused by being medicated to adjust a person's emotional state is how often people have difficulty drawing close to the Lord whether in worship or in private times. Their soul which is responsible for the emotional issues is being controlled by the medication rather than being led by their spirit. They will only be able to draw so close to the Lord while the soul is influenced so heavily by a drug.

While attempting to stabilize the emotional reaction to life they are only able to draw so close to other people as well. This is because they are using the meds to try to level off their emotions rather than feel bound and drug into what feels like the emotional drowning they cannot control. The purpose of the meds is to keep them from going so high or so low. It depends on what has caused them the need to seek help to stabilize. This keeps them from bottoming out.

This is also why many people want to get off the medications they are taking for emotional issues. I had a good friend who was undergoing treatment due to despair and depression in his life. Within four weeks he told me, "I have to get off these things. I can't get close to the Lord in worship the way I want to because the meds keep me from emotionally responding to God." Do you know that emotions are God given? They are part of the image of God and are part of who we are. The reason they take the meds in the first place is the desperation just to feel normal.

When we feel normal we do not think much about it. But when someone's emotions have so run amok, so taken over that they cannot function normally, they become desperate to somehow climb out of that despair. This is often the main reason they reach out to be medicated. They want to feel normal again.

If you are wondering if God can help them, the answer is yes. But when someone has grown to depend more heavily on their emotions than on God it is very difficult to trust God instead of their emotions. The emotions keep dragging them down.

This book is about learning to control our emotions. In the mean time have mercy and grace for people whose emotional state finds them in a pit, and they need to be encouraged and loved. They need to know that God still loves them, and so does the body of Christ. The tendency of those who have not gone through a valley of deep darkness is to question the need for this treatment. The reason for pursuing this type of treatment is they are in desperation.

Still, God is real. God is able to teach us to train our emotions to fall in line under Holy Spirit. We must understand that the enemy of our soul wants to destroy us. His attacks against people are most often directed at the soul.

They are ruthless, they are unrelenting and they use powerful weapons of destruction in order to rob us of God's glory that resides within us. There is a song with lyrics that should resonate within us. They speak of God and say, "He's real; He's real. Faith's a lot stronger than what you feel."

I believe a major part of our issues with medicating people is that we need to develop our faith and trust in God because He is a lot stronger than the feelings that can take over in our lives. I have a friend who enjoyed drinking diet Coke. He would drink 6-7 cans of diet Coke a day. By the time he would come home from work he was struggling with acid reflux. It felt like this habit was making everything rough and raw inside. His wife felt it was due to how much he was drinking soda pop, so he went to the doctor to find out if there was some way he could get rid of his physical issue without having to change his habit.

The doctor told him that if he did not want to change his habit he could give him a little purple pill which could take care of the acid reflux. This would allow him to continue to daily consume the amount of soda pop he enjoyed. He opted to medicate himself rather than change his liquid diet. The pill for him seemed to be more about medicating his pain than stopping the damage being done. Anything done in excess, in this case it was all the soda pop he was consuming, will cause one's body to say, "This isn't right." We can either listen to our bodies, which God created or we can tell our body to shut up by popping a pill.

I know about this type of physical issue personally as I used to drink coffee like it was going out of style. In the morning I would get up and have several cups. I loved to drink coffee. In the evening we would make a full pot, usually decaf, and my wife would drink a cup and I would finish the rest of the coffee we had brewed. After years of consuming more coffee than was good for my body I developed acid reflux.

I was made aware of what caused my problem when I talked with a friend who was coffee crazy. She received fifty pounds of coffee on her fortieth birthday from people. She was given all this wonderful coffee at a time her doctor had just told her that if she was going to continue to sing professionally she would need to stop drinking coffee. All the coffee she was drinking was causing such a bad case of acid reflux that she was not able to sing. She had been given a choice. She could continue with her coffee consumption or she could do what God had gifted her to do.

She chose to give up the coffee. As soon as she shared this with me, God's Spirit told me that this was my problem. So, I gave up the coffee. Not everybody is able to do that cold turkey, but that is what God told me to do, and it is what I needed to do.

Our tendency though is to go to the doctor and ask for something to fix it. We just want to fix it not take the time to deal with the problem. Often we have been doing something over a period of time where our emotions have enlarged their influence or our bodies are telling us this is not healthy for us. We want to medicate it instead of asking the Lord for the best answer because sometimes we do not want to hear God tell us what is wrong. We just want to keep doing what we are doing.

Sometimes people seek out Christian counselors who tell them what they need to do to make things right, but they do not want to hear it. They want to keep doing exactly what they are doing. People tend to take the easy road in life. Most would rather choose to deaden the pain in their life in order to make their life easier rather than deal with the issues that make life difficult. The more a person takes the easy road, the harder life will become.

If you take the easy road it usually goes down hill making it easier than the tougher road. Yet at some point you have to go back up hill or you will be stuck at the bottom. You have to find a way to come back up to the place in life God intends for you to live. If however you are always moving downward then getting back up where you belong eventually seems so far away. The tendency is to walk down hill on the easy path rather than determining to walk up a more difficult path. We have to realize what seems the more difficult path is where the children of God, the princes and princesses of the King of glory, are supposed to be living. We need to get back on the narrow path because God has so much more for us we will be missing if we stay on the wide and easy path that leads to a downward spiral.

The easy road does not take faith. One does not have to trust God to take the easy road. You just jump in the wagon and ride it to the bottom. Yet at some point on the journey you will start circling the emotional drain.

This is why choosing to walk close to God now by honoring the covenant He has made with you will make life easier because of your growing dependency on God. We are supposed to be depending on God. The more we depend on God the stronger we become. There will be times we have to take the more difficult road to get to the place God wants us. To take that road we have to walk with Jesus.

I know a young man whose parent put him on medication for ADHD as an elementary student because that was the counsel she had received. His testimony is that as he grew into his teens he needed medication to feel normal. Eventually those medications and some painful issues that came into his life led him to illegal drugs and alcohol. Sometimes the meds are not what is best for us; sometimes they are just what are easiest.

There is a stronghold that draws us to what is easiest based on our emotions. When we give in to them so much, those emotions become the controlling factor in our lives. I believe emotions have become the controlling factor in the Church. This can be seen by the ways the Church has chosen to do so many things the easier way. The Church needs to deal with her issues that cause the pain and learn to control her emotions or else we are going to pay the price of allowing our emotions to control us.

One summer my parents, my brother's family and my family went to Maui. While on the island we decided to take the Road to Hāna. According to Wikipedia, although Hāna is only about 52 miles from Kahului, a typical trip to Hāna takes about three hours, as the road is very winding, very narrow and passes over 59 bridges. Forty six of these are only one-lane bridges, requiring oncoming traffic to yield and occasionally causing brief traffic jams if two vehicles meet head-on. There are approximately 620 curves along Highway 360 from just east of Kahului to Hāna, virtually all of it through lush, tropical rainforest. (Information gathered from Wikipedia: Road to Hana.)

Some of our family members wanted to see the Road to Hāna without experiencing car sickness and chose to use travel medication in order to enjoy the long ride. Toward the end of the Road to Hāna is a beautiful place to stop and take pictures. The famous Seven Sacred Pools which were originally known as Oheo Gulch. Located in the Haleakala National Park this series of waterfalls and seven pools eventually leads into the Pacific Ocean. At the last pool is a group of rocks that people are warned not to jump off into the pool, but many people choose to jump off anyway. My brother who wanted to have the "full Maui experience" as he called it started jumping off the rocks into the pool with the others.

Those family members who had taken the travel medication never were able to see the pools because the meds had knocked them out. When my brother arrived and jumped out of the car he was saying "We're here, we're here!" But they were out of it. Sometimes the meds steal the experiences of life. While the concern about car sickness was real, the concern that one pill was not enough caused some of

103

our family members to take two pills. While having a really good nap, they missed out on a lot of beauty and fun.

It is a tendency we have to take meds in order to make our lives easier or feel better. These meds are designed to only mask the pain in our souls without dealing with the pain or the issues that cause the pain. While making it easier to control the pain, they do not rid us of the pain. This pain needs to be released by dealing with it. It is instead pushed down deeper in people's lives.

Most of the issues in people's lives are spiritual. Because people do not want to deal with issues spiritually they come up with other things to deal with and other reasons things are in their lives. People often medicate themselves because they do not want to take the more difficult road that will actually help bring healing to their lives. It is not the easiest thing to do. People have to deal with the issue in order to overcome the issue. They have to deal with the issue to resolve the emotions that are being faced. If one chooses not to deal with the issues, the emotions do not just go away. They may be hidden by the meds, but they are still there. They are still working to control how one lives and what one does.

People who are addicted to alcohol or drugs are addicted because they are trying to kill some kind of pain in their life. When young people party and get drunk it is not simply because they are having fun. Every one of them has spiritual issues in their heart and life that God wants to heal that are being masked by the alcohol or drugs. It will not change with age alone. While attending a thirty year High School Class Reunion, some of the people were still doing the same things they did in High School. They still had not dealt with the pain in their lives they acquired when they were younger and they had added more issues.

There are three truths that need to be grasped in order to overcome the "medicate it" disorder. The first one is God wants to be our healer. People have not been taught this or simply do not believe that God wants to be our healer. Two verses in Deuteronomy 28 demonstrate this. Earlier in the chapter God has used Moses to explain how He wanted to bless the Children of Israel if they would have fully obeyed and followed Him. Then He started to explain a series of consequences He was going to bring into their lives if they were to walk away from obeying and following Him. God explained that each time they moved further away He would do more and more to get their attention.

There are some who think if God really loved them He would not do this. But He does this to draw us back to Himself because of His love for us. In verses 27-28 Moses said "The LORD will smite you with the boils of Egypt and with tumors and with the scab and with the itch, from which you cannot be healed. The LORD will smite you with madness and with blindness and with *bewilderment of heart* . . . ." (Italics added.)

Then in verses 65-67 he says, "Among those nations you shall find no rest, and there will be no resting place for the sole of your foot; but there the LORD will give you *a trembling heart, failing of eyes, and despair of soul.*" And you will medicate it. Moses did not say that, but isn't that what people do today?

"So your life shall hang in doubt before you; and you will be in dread night and day, and shall have no assurance of your life. In the morning you shall say, 'Would that it were evening!' And at evening you shall say, 'Would that it were morning!' because of the dread of your heart which you dread, and for the sight of your eyes which you will see."

If you look in the book of Exodus you will realize that what Moses was teaching in Deuteronomy to the second generation of those who had been delivered from Egypt was based in the book of Exodus. In Exodus 15 the people had been crying out to God because the water they had to drink was bitter. So God cleaned the water, tested their hearts and declared this truth.

"If you will give earnest heed to the voice of the LORD your God, and do what is right in His sight, and give ear to His commandments, and keep all His statutes, I will put none of the diseases on you which I have put on the Egyptians; for *I, the LORD, am your healer.*"

There are four conditions God points out for the Lord to be our healer. The first one is that we listen carefully to the voice of God. The second is to do what is right in God's eyes; not what is right in our eyes. Not what our emotions tell us what to do, but what God sees as right. The third point is to pay attention to His commands and the fourth point is to keep all His decrees. If we do follow these four conditions we will know Him as the God who heals us.

Too often we do not listen for His voice. We run instead to medicate us from His voice. Too often we do not do what is right in God's eyes and something happens in our lives bringing worries and concerns, so we choose to medicate ourselves when God wants to heal us. Too often we do not pay attention to His commands or keep His decrees so we do not experience God's healing.

In Matthew 4:23 Jesus is an example of how God wants to heal us. Do you want to be like Jesus? Do you want to see this happening not just in your life but also in the lives of others? "Jesus was going throughout all Galilee, teaching in their synagogues and proclaiming the gospel (good news) of the kingdom . . . ."

In verse 17 it tells us what the good news of the Kingdom is. "From that time Jesus began to preach and say, 'Repent, for the kingdom of heaven is at hand.'" The word repent is from two Greek words meaning to change the way one thinks about something. That is Jesus' message about the good news of the Kingdom.

Jesus was healing every kind of disease and every kind of sickness among the people. "Then they brought to Him all who were ill, those suffering with various diseases and pains, demoniacs, epileptics, paralytics; and He healed them." Then in Luke 6:17-19 there is a similar account: "Jesus came down with them and stood on a level place; and there was a large crowd of His disciples, and a great throng of people from all Judea and Jerusalem and the coastal region of Tyre and Sidon, who had come to hear Him and to be healed of their diseases; and those who were troubled with unclean spirits were being cured. And all the people were trying to touch Him, for power was coming from Him and healing them all."

We turn away from God because we just do not trust God. It may not be a big issue that causes someone to turn away. Galatians 6:1 says that if someone is caught in something they did not deliberately do, they just fell into it. Like hitting a patch of ice and sliding into a ditch. It says a spiritual person should restore them. Sometimes we want to walk with God but we do something we did not want to do. That is what this verse is talking about. Then those who are spiritual are supposed to restore someone like this with a spirit of gentleness because you do not know if it will happen to you. God wants us out there restoring people, not judging them for what happens.

Do you remember in Daniel 4 when because of his pride King Nebuchadnezzar was driven out of his kingdom to eat grass like an animal? When the seven year period of time was over he recalled: "at the end of that period, I, Nebuchadnezzar, raised my eyes toward heaven and my reason returned to me, and I blessed the Most High and praised and honored Him."

People believe that medicating will control our problems but most problems are spiritually related problems which are caused by out of balanced souls. Souls through emotions are in more control of what is going on than is one's spirit. It is through one's spirit that a human is able to connect with Holy Spirit. When we are connected with Holy Spirit, the emotions we have are the emotions God wants us to have.

The second truth is that we need to develop and grow our spirit to receive greater things from Holy Spirit. Picture your soul and spirit each having the opportunity to go to a gym where there is a trainer that is going to develop them. They are going to grow stronger; they are going to grow bigger. Which one would you rather control, grow and feed your spirit or your soul? Hopefully your spirit because the larger your spirit becomes the smaller is the control of your soul over you. The more we feed our soul our spirit gets smaller and the voice of God has less influence in our lives.

My friend Doug Heck shared some thoughts with me about growing our spirits larger. I realized when we allow our emotions to control us our soul grows larger than our spirit. In Genesis 3 Adam and Eve were in the Garden of Eden. Eve had been tempted by Satan to doubt God. Doubting is an emotional response. Both Eve and Adam gave in to the temptation, their eyes were opened, they realized they were naked, sewed fig leaves together and they tried to hide from God. What was natural, after having allowed sin into their lives, suddenly caused them to begin to experience shame and guilt. Then in verse 8 we find out "they heard the sound of the LORD God walking in the garden in the cool of the day, and the man and his wife hid themselves from the presence of the LORD God among the trees of the garden."

Adam and Eve chose to listen to their souls over their spirits. They began to doubt God and their souls became a little bigger. They lost the one thing that had kept them in communion with God. Where verse 8 spoke of them hearing the sound of the Lord, the Hebrew word literally said the "voice" of the Lord. God was speaking to them in the Garden. As God walked in the garden it reads "in the cool of the day." The phrase translated "in the cool" is the

Hebrew word which means "spirit". If you read the passage in its literal translation it reads "they heard the voice of the Lord God walking in the garden in the spirit that day." That is how God speaks to us, in our spirit.

They hid among the trees of the garden from the presence of the Lord. Do we still do that today? Hear the voice of God and rather than respond with our spirit do we hide behind things? "God I'm really busy right now. Let me just finish this." Sometimes the Lord will speak when we are having our time alone with Him and we are so busy reading a passage that we tell Him, "I just have to finish this chapter and then I'm good to listen." In that moment God wants us to put the Bible down and listen to what He has to say to us.

Adam and Eve were hiding behind the trees because they were dealing with the feeling of guilt. They had done something they were not supposed to do. They were afraid (another emotion) and ashamed (another emotion) so they would not come out and talk to the Lord God who had come walking through the garden in the Spirit speaking to them. God speaks to us in our spirit and the larger our spirit grows the smaller our soul grows. You only have room for your spirit or your soul to grow larger in your body.

Either your spirit will grow bigger and you will trust God in more and for more things or your soul will grow larger and your spirit will grow smaller. We need to grow our spirits so we are more sensitive to God and we hear Him more clearly in order to do what He wants us to do.

If our choice is to listen to our emotions and our soul above listening to the Spirit and allowing our emotions to respond to the Spirit of God then our soul will grow bigger. Eventually we will find ourselves in a place where we think we need to medicate ourselves because our soul will be saying "You have so much pain, cover it up so you do not have to deal with it and no one will see it. You have so many issues in your life, but you can get through life on your own."

Rather than going to God who says to us, "Let me just take the pain and heal you so you do not have to deal with it anymore."

Our soul often responds with – "But Lord, that is going to take work. I may need other people's help and I really don't want to get other people involved with my life because if they see who I am they might not love me or like me anymore."

Unfortunately, that has been the case in Jesus' Church far too long. Romans 12:10 tells us to be devoted to one another in brotherly love and to honor each other above ourselves. If we did this more, I am convinced people would come to the people of Jesus Christ more for healing. Instead they feel like they are going to be judged by us.

The question is "are you growing your spirit or are you feeding your soul?" Every time we give in to our souls they get a little bigger. Every time we give in to our spirits and our spirits are aligned with Holy Spirit our spirits grow larger. Every time we want to give in to our spirits but we think someone else might not like it and we get pulled back over to a reaction of our soul. It is because we need to choose to trust God. Even if someone else does not like what God wants me to do, I would rather be who God wants me to be, than what everybody else wants. Wouldn't you much rather have your spirit grow and become who God says you are than allow your soul to keep pulling you back to what you were? Of course you would!

Our goal should be that we are so in touch with Holy Spirit that we can face issues or help other people face issues. It is not just about us getting healed. One of the reasons God heals us is so we will help others get healed, to help other people become set free. Jesus said that freely we have received so freely we should give – that includes our spiritual, emotional and physical healings.

The third truth is that as we trust God to be spiritually healed of our emotional needs, we will help others. Once we have been healed we have something that we can use to help others deal with their issues so they do not have to medicate themselves to get by. Every time I see God extend or grow someone's leg that is shorter than their other leg, I have a growing trust and faith that God will do it the next time as well. The reason why; I have seen Him do it already. I have seen God heal people's backs. I know He can do it. Every time you have seen God provide for you in some way, you know He is able to do it next time. Now you can take what you know to be true and share it with a world that does not know it is true, that does not have hope, and that desperately needs someone to point out the spiritual issues that are involved which may have been blocked out of their lives. God has not forgotten them. God is speaking to them and He wants to draw them close to Him.

Armed with that kind of help we can minister freedom to people inside and outside the Church. You can minister freedom to people through your relationship with Jesus Christ. It is time for us to understand how that works. We need to deal first with the issues of our lives that we have been suppressing or hiding because God wants to heal us. Once we have been healed by God we need to realize that God has put us in places and all kinds of relationships with people who need to be healed. Wherever God has placed you is where you are a minister.

You may teach a Sunday School class; you may have a job outside the local congregation; you may work with a little league team; with young people, or you may be directed by God as you are shopping or drinking coffee. Wherever you are, with whomever is present, you need to realize that God has placed you sovereignly there to bring healing to a life that has been taught and trained to medicate themselves and not look to God for His healing power.

In order to minister more effectively we need to understand how to grow our spirits larger. Let me ask you, do you believe that God gives love, joy, peace, patience, kindness, goodness, faithfulness, gentleness, and self-control – the fruit of the Spirit? Then ask God for these as these are the things that grow your spirit.

Let me challenge you to sit down today and write out five examples from your life of how you overcame your emotions and made right decisions, the spiritual decisions God wanted you to make. These do not have to be big major life changing decisions. They can be everyday examples of your choosing to live in the Spirit rather than reacting with your emotions. This will help you see that you are already moving in God's Spirit to do those things. If you can only come up with two examples it will tell you that there are some major things that need to be changed in your life.

Another way to grow your spirit is by choosing to walk and talk with God. Do this by reading your Bible. Do this by getting around people who have a passion for God and want to grow their spirits as well, instead of being around people who want their soul to grow. These people will talk about God and want to see you do the same. I have a sign in my office that says "My closest friends are those who motivate my thirst for God." Those are the types of people who should be your closest friends if you are choosing to grow your spirit.

You will recognize these people right away by how their decisions are made. Do not judge people who want to grow their soul. Get with people who want their spirit to grow. Show up at Bible Studies; show up at worship times, show up to let God move in your life. Do not show up just to watch what is going on. Be an active participant in what God is doing and respond when people challenge you to take action that helps you draw closer to God.

If you need to overcome something that is an issue of your life, whether it is fear or something else, you may need to meet with people to have them pray specifically for your release from that issue. You can sit down with anyone who is walking closely with God and pray through the issues of your heart that are causing your soul to give in to your emotions instead of your spirit.

Commit to minister in the marketplace where you work and live. Commit to take it outside the walls of the local congregation. What you know already should be made available to help others. There are already people in your life that you can help by sharing and praying with them about the power of God to heal them.

One of our friends who started a property development and building business determined that they were not just going to build houses but they were going to build God into the houses. They call and talk with county employees about property and permits in relationship to their business and God opens doors for them to pray and minister in the employee's lives over the phone. When they meet with subcontractors or people interested in building a home they make a point to pray for them and with them.

This is one example of how God's people can help people begin to step out of the "medicate it" disorder by praying with people and seeing the release of the power of God to change lives. You may not know it yet, but you are ready to move in this way. If that makes you nervous, know that it is my responsibility to make you uncomfortable so you will draw closer and closer to God, to learn to rely more and more on Him. May God bless you richly as you go out today to demonstrate for people God's power to heal and release them from their dependency on meds rather than depending on God.

## Chapter 6

# The "Lowering The Bar" Syndrome

Did you know that there are people who are able to clear a crossbar that is eight feet high in some track and field competitions? If anyone has competed in the track and field event called the "high jump" or watched someone else compete they know that the flexible bar that they have attempted to jump over is the horizontal crossbar. Do you know how they determine what the starting height is for the high jump bar at each event? According to an email I received from the International Association of Athletes Federation (IAAF) Competitions Department, "The starting height obviously depends on the quality of the participants and should be low enough to allow the weakest of athletes entered to be able to make at least one successful jump. The athlete's best or average performance during the season should be taken as a reference."

So the crossbar is set at a certain height predetermined by what would allow the weakest competitor to clear the bar at least once and each time an athlete is able to clear the bar or jump higher than the bar without knocking it off the stands it rests on, the bar is raised a little higher. Once the bar has been established at a height for competition, the bar is not lowered during that competition.

Let's take a look at what the starting point is for the spiritual bar in our lives, how we lower the bar and how we can keep the bar at the right height. Too many of us spend time lowering the spiritual bar in our lives rather than keeping it where it belongs.

The lowering of the bar syndrome is when we allow for insignificance in the guise of inclusiveness letting people stay the same and get their own way. Another way to say this is we do not want people to feel bad about themselves for their efforts so we include them while allowing them to stay the same. We are at the same time allowing them to have their own way without ever accomplishing what they are supposed to accomplish. We do not want them to feel bad so we lower the bar to where they are. When we allow for insignificance, which means without importance or meaningless, we lower the bar as Christians so that people are insignificant and what they do is unimportant for God.

Jesus does not lower the bar. The spiritual bar is set at a certain height and throughout the Bible Jesus never lowers the bar. In Mark 10 a man ran up to Jesus and asked Him what he needed to do to inherit eternal life. Jesus shared six biblical commands with the man. The six commands included: Do not murder, do not commit adultery, do not steal, do not bear false witness, do not defraud, and honor your father and mother. The man responded to Jesus by claiming that he had kept all six of these commands since he was a boy.

Keep in mind that in Matthew chapter 5 Jesus had taught that anyone who murdered was liable to the court. Then He took this command further by saying anyone who even got angry with his brother was guilty before the court. Jesus explained that if someone looked at a woman with lust for her then he had already committed adultery in his heart with her. Jesus had said not to lie, not to defraud (which is giving something to someone that is not yours to give), and to honor his father and mother. Now with our propensity to sin, including stretching the truth, there is probably not anyone who has kept all these commands.

Jesus looked at the man and loved him and because He loved him, He did not chew Him out. He did not ask for a word of knowledge to point out to the man times in his life where he had not kept all of these commands. Instead Jesus looked at him and loved him. He chose what was best for the man because love is an act of self sacrifice for the good of another. Even though Jesus loved him; Jesus could not, Jesus would not lower the bar. Instead He said to him "One thing you lack: go and sell all you possess and give to the poor, and you will have treasure in heaven; and come, follow Me."

There was just one thing he had to do. Jesus knew his heart. He looked at this young man and He knew this man loved his possessions more than he loved God. He loved his riches more than he loved God so Jesus put him on the spot by challenging him to give up the one thing that the man treasured and loved more than anything else in his life. Not only did Jesus test his heart by saying sell it all, but he than challenged him to give all the money to the poor and follow Jesus. Did you notice that the key to living correctly was and is to follow Jesus?

At this, the man's face fell; he was sad and grieved because he owned a lot of property and had a great deal of wealth. Jesus did not lower the bar, even though He loved him. He did not say "You know what, I'm thinking that if you give away ten percent of everything you own to the poor and come and follow me that would be a good starting point. Maybe in six months we'll have you give away another ten percent. Then over a period of time you will have gotten rid of all those things because your love for Father God will have grown so much."

That would have been lowering the bar. Instead Jesus kept the bar at the same level and told the man he had to come up to the bar. The bar you see was set at one level. He had to love God more than he loved anything else. It is still at the same level today.

Then Jesus made the statement "How hard it will be for those who are wealthy to enter the kingdom of God!" and the disciples were totally amazed at that statement. They asked who can be saved if the rich people find it so hard to be saved. Jesus said, "Children, how hard it is to enter the kingdom of God! It is easier for a camel to go through the eye of a needle than for a rich man to enter the Kingdom of God."

When I was little, my mom would sew clothing we had torn while playing. I would watch her take that little thread and stick it through the eye of a needle. At some point in her life she needed glasses to be able to put the thread through the eye of the needle she was using. If her glasses were not right there near where she was working she would call one of us over to thread the needle for her. I always thought that was what Jesus was talking about when he talked about a camel going through the eye of a needle.

It would be impossible for a full size camel to go through the eye of a sewing needle. There are reports that there was a gate in the city of Jerusalem that was considered the Needle's Eye. There supposedly was a large city gate with a small door in it about four feet high. The only way to get a camel through the gate would have been to unload the camel, taking everything off of it and then have the camel get down on its knees and crawl through the gate.

How hard it was for a camel to go through the eye of a needle, much less a rich person to make it into the Kingdom of God. It is not impossible, but what He was saying in relationship to this particular rich man was he loved his wealth more than he loved God. That was why it was so hard.

I know of people who are wealthy who love God far above their wealth. People who love their wealth more than they love God are compared to a camel that would be forced to try to crawl on its knees through a gate called the Needle's Eye. After taking everything off the camel, it still would take a while to get the camel through the gate. With this rich man, he needed to take all his love of wealth off by selling it and giving it to the poor in order to enter God's Kingdom. This was a picture for them and for us today of how much we need to love God.

Jesus did not say the man's issue was insignificant or unimportant. It was instead of such high importance it was compared to eternal life. Nevertheless, Jesus was not going to lower the bar for him by saying, "You don't have to do that. It's enough for you just to follow Me," Jesus knew his heart. There are times since God knows our hearts so well that between God and us we hear His voice say to us, "You need to do this." Then as we struggle with God we ask the question, "Am I going to love you so much God that I will do what you have told me to do?"

This is about when you know what God wants you to do. Do you love Him enough to do it? A stronghold that is faced so many times with the lowering of the bar syndrome is apathy. We do not really think it matters so we lower the bar. People have tendency to weaken the intensity of truth in order to make it user friendly. In order to let people in under the bar we say, "You don't have to do all that, just start to do this."

Where does the primary height of the spiritual bar start? According to the IAAF in track and field competition, it should be as low as it takes to let the weakest participant clear it once. But the spiritual bar has a starting place that it cannot be any lower than, as far as God is concerned. The starting place of the spiritual bar is loving God. That is where the bar is at, you have to love God. You have to love Him above everything else. That is where the bar is at. That is what Christianity is all about. That is what your relationship with God is all about. We are to love God with all our heart, soul, mind and strength – the greatest commandment.

It is not what you do. It is not that you have to show up to worship with others every Sunday although that is a really good thing. But where the bar is set is different. The bar cannot be lowered to attending on Sunday. It is not whether you tithe. It is not whether you share Jesus with people, it is not how many miracles you have done; it is simply loving God. That is where the bar is set.

Some people will try to raise the bar higher than that by saying you have to do a list of activities, of dos and don'ts. That is not where God has put the bar. People may have placed the bar there, but God put the bar where everybody can reach it, and that is loving Him. Does that take some effort? Yes it does, but it is attainable for anyone.

In Deuteronomy 30:11-14 Moses told the Children of Israel: "For this commandment which I command you today is not too difficult for you, nor is it out of reach. It is not in heaven, that you should say, ' Who will go up to heaven for us to get it for us and make us hear it, that we may observe it?' Nor is it beyond the sea, that you should say, 'Who will cross the sea for us to get it for us and make us hear it, that we may observe it?' But the word is very near you, in your mouth and in your heart, that you may observe it."

The bar is set at an attainable height for everyone. It is in your mouth and in your heart. If we would focus on this, everything else would fall into place in our lives. Should we put our love in other things, in ourselves, in other people then we choose to lower the bar. If we love other things, ourselves or other people more than we love God that is when we lower the bar. But God never lowers the bar below loving Him.

People think it cannot be that easy. They do not believe that all they have to do is love God with all their heart, soul, mind and strength and that is all God expects of them? Yes that is all. Do you know why that is all God expects of us? Because if we love God that much, then we will do whatever He says; we will do whatever He wants. So if we could focus on loving God that way then all the other commandments will fall into place under that. Everything else God would ask you to do you would not even hesitate. You would respond to Him with, "God I love you, of course I will do that for you. Of course, I will do that for you!"

The way we determine where the bar has been set is the greatest commandment to love the Lord our God. Do you know how the Bible defines love? Love is more than an emotion. Love is a choice. In the Old Testament the Hebrew word for love placed greater emphasis on the choosing of something or someone than it did on the emotional response toward something or someone. It was 90% choosing and 10% emotion. When God said He loved Jacob but He hated Esau in the book of Genesis, God was talking about choosing Jacob and not choosing Esau for His plan to father a great nation.

Yet we have so allowed emotions to define everything in our lives we think everything is about our emotions. While my wife and I were counseling a young married couple the young man told me, "I have come to realize that to love her means I have to choose her. I have to choose what is best for her above what is best for me. I always want the infatuation the rest of my life but love is my choice of what is best for her."

People today think love is that warm feeling we have. When I was younger, people used to call it "puppy love" as though that could have explained away the impact of choosing someone at a young age. It may have been puppy love but it was real to the puppies. The warm feeling is the infatuation; love is the choice, the day to day choice. Anyone who has been married knows the difference between loving their spouse and liking them. Friends may do something that upsets us enough that we do not like them that day, but we still love them. We still choose them to be our friends.

With God you have to choose to do what is best for God all the time if you love Him, just like He does for you. In the New Testament there are two different words used for love. One means brotherly love that is a camaraderie or companion type love. The other is a love that God says we are supposed to share with each other as Christians because we are part of the same spiritual family. This love is an unconditional love which is displayed by acts of self sacrifice for the good of another. This definition is based on John 3:16. "For God so loved the world that He gave His only begotten Son . . . ." God demonstrated His love by giving His Son as an act of self sacrifice for us. He chose us.

In John 14:21 Jesus said, "If you love me, I'll love you and Father God will love you and I'll reveal myself to you." So love is all about a choice. When we talk about the bar being at a certain height, it is our choosing God above everything else in our lives? We choose God above our families, we choose God above our friends, we choose God above our jobs; we even choose God above where we are going to live. There are more and more people who have been sharing that God moved them to a specific city or town. One couple shared how God moved them from Vancouver, WA, to Vantage, WA and then God moved them to Coeur de lane, ID.

God moves pastors from local congregation to local congregation every year. Rarely though does one hear of people who are not in full time ministry moved to another location because they recognized that God wanted them to move to be part of what He was doing in another place. Some have not realized the new job they have taken requiring a move was the hand of God relocating them to advance the

Kingdom of Heaven. People should love God so much that when He says to move, they respond by moving. There are people who have moved and have not been sure why they moved other than God told them to move.

A couple Bonnie and I have met moved from east of the Mississippi River to Moses Lake, WA and were asking God a few months later why He had them move to Moses Lake? They had thought God was moving them to Vancouver, WA, but on the trip out while stopping in Moses Lake God told them to stay there. God moves people without them knowing why or where they are going. These people are so in love with God they have the attitude, "God if that is what you want, we are there!"

If the phrase "we love God more than our family" makes people nervous, that is what Jesus said. He said: "If you love your father, your mother, your sister or your brother more than Me, then you have missed it." (that is the RJS paraphrase of Matthew 10:37). If you are thinking that does not sound right, it does not sound like what Jesus would say, then take out your Bible and read Matthew 10:37 again. Because the bar is set at loving God and if you love your family members more than God, you have lowered the bar by living a lifestyle that has told God that He is not as important to you as He should be. Keep the bar at the level God has set it, for if you love Him then He will give you the power to love your family with His unconditional love. He will give you the strength to love your family and want what is best for your family members.

Where the bar is set is the spiritual issue in our lives. When we lower the bar for people while thinking we are helping them, it will in reality make matters worse for them. They will not reach where God wants them to reach. They will not become who God has made them to be. Sometimes as strange as this may sound, people let their emotions keep them from loving God.

In 2 Chronicles 14 King Asa had to trust God because an army larger than his own had come against Judah and King Asa cried out to the Lord saying, "LORD, there is no one like you to help the powerless against the mighty. Help us, O LORD our God, for we rely on you, and in your name we have come against this vast army. O LORD, you are our God; do not let man prevail against you." NIV

When a large army came against this king and his people he cried out to God for help and God helped him by striking down this army. It is recorded that "Such a great number of Cushites fell that they could not recover; they were crushed before the LORD and his forces. The men of Judah carried off a large amount of plunder." NIV

King Asa saw God wipe out a huge army, yet when you get to chapter 16 some twenty five years later the king of Israel came against him and this time he decided to take the silver and gold out of the Lord's temple to send as a gift to another king while seeking protection rather than asking God for His help. Why would someone do that? When they have seen God do the miraculous by having protected and taken care of them, why would they take what God had given to them for His glory and sell it out to someone else to protect them? Why not trust God to do again what they had seen God do in the past? This was a king of Judah, why would he do that?

The prophet Hanani came to King Asa in chapter 16 verse 8 and asked him, "Were not the Ethiopians and the Lubim an immense army with very many chariots and horsemen? Yet because you relied on the LORD, He delivered them into your hand."

Then in verse 9 we read, "For the eyes of the LORD move to and fro throughout the earth that He may strongly support those whose heart is completely His. You have acted foolishly in this. Indeed, from now on you will surely have wars."

King Asa had trusted God the first time and God had wiped out the enemy. But years later as he had settled into being comfortable, as he had settled into not being willing to go to war when God wanted him to go to war, instead of trusting God as He had the first time, this king gave away the articles from the temple of the God he said he trusted. He gave these things to another king who he asked to protect him.

As a result God sent a prophet to him who told him, "Man did you blow it!" He had the opportunity to trust the same God he had trusted 25 years earlier. "Man did you blow it!" Rather than repenting (changing the way he thought) and allowing God to restore the blessing in his life King Asa was so angry, so enraged that he put Hanani in prison and began "to oppress some of his own people."

When God's people do not do what God wants in this way, when we have seen the Lord take care of us and we choose a different direction, we become angry. Not only do we get mad at the person God has sent to correct us, we take our anger out on others as well. Think about the lives in which you have seen this happen. You have been impressed by people who have stood with God and months or years later something has happened. The passion for God is gone and the fire has burned out. All that seems to be left is like a burned out camp fire where you find smoldering wood. The fire for God is gone; there is no passion for Jesus which results in the decision for them to do it their own way. They have decided to do it a different way than God wants.

While watching this take place in their lives a person comes who has been sent by God to help them stir the passion for God up again. Instead you have seen them get mad at the person God has sent to help them. They have reacted with the attitude who are you to tell me what I should do? As a result they begin to oppress and get angry with other people who love Jesus, who have a passion for their God. That is what happens when a person lowers the bar.

King Asa's fear took over instead of relying on his trust and love for God. By lowering the bar King Asa was saying "I know God took care of me 25 years ago, but I don't think He can do it this time. I'm going to trust somebody else." When God says to love Him and He will take care of you yet you choose to trust another, do you see how that is lowering the bar?

Rather than control our emotions we tend to think and say, "It's okay to feel that way. It's okay when someone says they won't forgive someone else to feel that way." Believers in Jesus even say things like, "Its okay, in time you will be able to forgive that person." When we encourage people to harbor their anger, their unforgiveness; we have lowered the bar. Jesus said that we are supposed to forgive people and instead of taking the time to help someone work through their hurt and forgive, we lower the bar and tell them it is okay for them to do what Jesus Christ has told us is wrong to do. God does not give us the option of not forgiving someone.

In Matthew 18 Jesus told a parable about the kingdom of heaven. The parable was about two servants who were in debt. The first was in debt to a king and the second was in debt to the first servant. The first servant owed the king a great deal of money. When the king called him to pay off his debt he could not afford to pay it back. He threw himself on the mercy of the king and pleaded for forgiveness. The king generously forgave the man's debt. Yet when the servant left the presence of the king he found the second servant and demanded from him a much smaller amount of money that the second servant owed the first. The second servant was in a financial position that kept him from being able to pay back the first servant, much like the position the first servant was in when the king had forgiven him. But the first servant refused to show mercy and had the second servant thrown in jail.

Then word came back to the king who called the first servant back in to his presence and declared to him, "'You wicked slave, I forgave you all that debt because you pleaded with me. Should you not also have had mercy on your fellow slave, in the same way that I had mercy on you?' And his lord, moved with anger, handed him over to the torturers until he should repay all that was owed him. Then Jesus said, 'My heavenly Father will also do the same to you, if each of you does not forgive his brother from your heart.'"

Jesus did not say eventually when you feel like it, He said we have to forgive. The first servant was not allowed to wait for a time until he felt like forgiving the second servant. The king required immediate forgiveness. Forgiveness is releasing someone else from our judgment. When we do not forgive another person we are judging them. We hold others in contempt, we do not believe they are worthy of forgiveness – that is judging them. There is far too much of this going on within the Church. It is why many people are being spiritually tormented in their life. It is time the people of God realize that if we do not forgive someone as freely as God has forgiven us; our problem is with God not with other people. When people choose not to forgive another person, they are lowering the bar of God's love.

"I love God, I obey God; I forgive people." We have to teach this to people. We especially have to teach our children this truth so that they walk in God's forgiveness too. Do we truly believe that God forgives us of anything we do if we confess our sin to Him? Did Jesus ask Father God to forgive those who beat Him and put Him on the cross? Do we truly want to be like Jesus? When we do not choose to forgive we have allowed our emotions to be in control of us rather than Holy Spirit.

A reason someone might not forgive someone is because their emotions are saying, "I have the right to be mad at them." People have shared horrible stories of what others did to them. They may have felt that they could never forgive them, yet when you talk and pray with them they are able to come to the place in their lives where they can say, "In the name of Jesus, I forgive." That is when the spiritual tormentors have to leave their lives. Those things that have been coming against their soul, spiritually beating on them, have to go and they are released in freedom as they forgive. We have to be people who forgive or we lower the bar.

When we do not love others we lower the bar. Jesus said "If you love me you will obey my commands." In John 4:19-21 we read, "We love, because He first loved us. If someone says, 'I love God,' and hates his brother, he is a liar; for the one who does not love his brother whom he has seen, cannot love God whom he has not seen. And this commandment we have from Him, that the one who loves God should love his brother also."

Loving someone means we have not lowered the bar for them. In Norm Willis' book Unity With A Return, he wrote: "A covenant simply means to bring together. It is the binding together of relationship broken by sin. Covenant is directed first of all toward God but not exclusively to Him. Whenever there is sin there is broken relationship and where there is broken relationship covenant is the means by which relationship is healed and brought back together, first toward God then with each other." Unity With A Return by Norm Willis p. 8. © Norm Willis. Published by Christ's Church Publishing, Kirkland, WA 98034. Used by permission

There is a lot of talk about covenant these days. When a person gives their life to Jesus they have come into covenant with God. It is a binding contract where the person says, "No matter what happens God, I know you will not walk away from me." On God's part He has given us principles of covenant that when we sin and walk away from God, we need to go back to God and confess our sin restoring our end of the covenant He has not broken. By making this covenant with God we are bound to God as individuals. The blood of Jesus sets us free to be bound to God. In coming into covenant with God we have come into covenant with each other.

The Church does not have unity today because we do not honor covenant with each other. Covenant is based on relationship and when that covenant is not honored people go around talking about others behind their back. Anger is allowed to fester and rather than go to the person one is angry with, they talk with someone else about the person. Grudges are held against each other and rather than forgiving and moving on, the choice of so many people is to go on talking with other people while spiritually shunning the person the grudge is being held against. By doing this people are breaking covenant with other people who they will spend eternity in heaven with because of choosing to emotionally respond to people rather that spiritually responding to them.

Norm also wrote: "The aim of walking covenantally is to preserve the unity of relationship in the heat of Satan's attacks in order that Father's desire for a mature bride can be fully realized." (ibid. p. 10) When the enemy attacks or when something takes place between two believers in Jesus Christ that causes them to come into a conflict of disunity, what binds us together to straighten things out is the covenant we have made with God and with each other.

A man who has been serving God for decades that had been a pastor, a missionary in Africa for years, and was leading a ministry at the time, told us that more than once other Christians had not loved him with a covenantal love but had hurt him instead. He had chosen not to come to a gathering the first time we had come to the city where he lived to explain the vision God had given us for taking the state of Washington because he compared us to snake oil salesmen who just wanted to get something from him. At the heart of why he would not come to listen was that he was unwilling to risk being hurt one more time. He was not going to give his time to it.

His wife went home from the gathering to explain to him what we called to do was not what he had thought. He called another pastor to ask him what he thought. He came the next time we were in the city and he realized that we did not come to get people to follow us. Instead we pointed out that it was not about us, but about God raising others up to be the people God had called them to be. It was about God calling people out to do what He had for them to do. It has resonated in the hearts of people as they recognize they are called to advance the Kingdom of Heaven. This brother was not used to someone coming with this message. Instead his heart was tired of people being disloyal to each other within the Church.

While in another city in our state there was a young man who pulled me aside to ask a question. "What's wrong with the Church?" he asked. "I have so many people that I know who will not go to Church anymore because the Church has hurt them in some way. What is wrong with the Church; is there any hope for her?"

The answer was, "Jesus is reviving His Church and He is her hope." People are part of the Church even if they do not belong to a local congregation, if they have given their life to Jesus Christ. The Church is who we all are. If there is a problem with the Church it is because there may be an infection in one of the body parts. Just like with our human body we cannot just cut off an arm and go on with life. The arm needs to be restored. That is what revival is, the restoration of the Church. It is the Spirit of God coming to change the hearts and lives of God's people so we love each other like Jesus told us to love each other. We have to stop lowering the bar by saying things like, "I don't like the way that person talked to me. I don't think I can fellowship with that person anymore because they have a different standard than I do."

Our family was in relationship with a couple who had a different philosophy of raising their children than we did. They came over one Halloween unannounced so our children could play games. The issue that caused them to withdraw from our relationship was that our children were dressed in costumes to go out and get candy. Now before you cast aside the remainder of this book because you may or may not allow your children to dress up on Halloween going door to door saying "Trick or Treat" and receiving candy, let me make my point. After that evening the young couple wanted nothing else to do with us. Our children could no longer play together. They always had a reason why we could not get together socially. We were in the same congregation together. We were on the staff of the same congregation. He was part of the Christian School staff, I was a member of the pastoral staff and we will spend eternity together fellowshipping in heaven. But they would have nothing to do with us.

It is time we stop treating each other that way and start loving each other the way Jesus loved and continues to love people. We are able to say to others, "Even if you disagree with me on that matter, I can still love you." There are going to be people in heaven that we are going to wonder how they got into heaven? They will be looking at us wondering how we got in, because here on earth we are not committed to covenant relationship with each other. That type of commitment says no matter what happens we are in the same spiritual family. We are in the family of God together and we share the same Heavenly Father.

I have two brothers and a sister and no matter what they have done, no matter how irritating they may have ever been to me – they are still my brothers and sister. No matter what I have ever done or said – I am still their brother. Anybody who has given their life to Jesus Christ, no matter whether they doctrinally agree with you, said something to you, or left a congregation you have been in fellowship with and you knew they were whacked out, they are still your brother or sister in Jesus. We have to start embracing each other and stop this attitude.

As we began traveling around the state of Washington sharing the vision of what God wants to do to take our state I brought with me copies of Norm Willis' book <u>Unity With A Return</u>. Let me recommend it to you. Norm writes convincingly of our need for unity based on our covenant relationship with each other. If you want a copy you will have to contact Christ's Church in Kirkland, WA for a copy. Their website is www.cckirkland.org and Christ's Church Publishing's phone number is (206) 820-2900.

To stop lowering the bar we have to establish it by loving God and if we love God we have to love all of the people who have given their lives to Jesus Christ like Jesus did and does. In the book <u>Love, Acceptance and Forgiveness</u> that Jerry Cook wrote a number of years ago he gave an example of what it means to be in covenant with each other that does not lower the bar of loving God by loving each other. "Love is commitment and it operates out of what we feel or do not feel. We need to extend this love to everyone who comes into our church: 'Brother, I want you to know that I'm committed to you. You'll never knowingly suffer at my hands. I'll never say or do anything, knowingly, to hurt you. I'll always in every circumstance seek to help you and support you. If you're down and I can lift you up, I'll do that. Anything I have that you need, I'll share with you; and if need be I'll give it to you. No matter what I find out about you and no matter what happens in the future, either good or bad, my commitment to you will never change. And there's nothing you can do about it. You don't have to respond. I love you, and that's what it means.'" Love, Acceptance and Forgiveness by Jerry Cook, p. 13, © Jerry Cook. Published by Gospel Light (or Regal), Ventura CA, 93003. Used by permission.

A number of years ago a pastor who I was friends with came into sharp disagreement with us about what was happening in our congregation's life situation. About three years later while walking through a local warehouse store we ended up on the same aisle face to face with each other. I walked up, gave him a hug and asked how things were going. He seemed taken back, but our conversation quickly picked up and we were able to talk with each other. I know that he loves Jesus and is going to be in heaven some day just as I will. Yet if I had lowered the bar, I would have chosen not to reach out to him in love even though we are in a covenant relationship through Jesus Christ our Lord. There are people who have walked out of our lives to whom we still need to demonstrate the love of Jesus.

We are finding as Holy Spirit examines our lives that we allow our emotions to keep us from loving each other. We allow our emotions to keep us from loving God. Most of us at some point became mad at God. We did not tell anyone we were mad at God because, you know . . . He is God. We have harbored in our hearts to some degree that God did not do right by us. I know people who have walked away from God because they felt He had not done what they thought He should have done. Something happened in their life that they are still upset at God for letting happen.

If you want to keep the bar from being lowered you have to keep the passion for God burning in your heart. I cannot light the fire in your heart, only God can light the fire, and you are responsible to stir up within you the passion for Him. Each of us needs to passionately be pursuing God or we will begin lowering the spiritual bar in our lives. When we stop pursuing God we stop making progress spiritually and the doors that God wants to open will stop opening for us because we have stopped advancing toward them. Let's commit to advance the Kingdom of God by passionately loving God and choosing not to lower the bar.

# Chapter 7

# The "Fighting For My Rights" Syndrome/Disorder

There are times when a can of frozen juice is opened, the contents are poured in a pitcher, three cans of water are added and then an additional portion of a can is added to make more of the juice. By adding too much water we may dilute the juice causing it to lose some of its flavor.

When we allow our emotions to take over in our lives that is what happens to us spiritually. We become diluted. We lose the flavor of God in our lives. As we see how emotions can be the source of so much of the control of our culture, be alert, keep your eyes wide open, be at the ready; do not allow your emotions to use any situation to slow you down in your pursuit of following after God by diluting your effectiveness.

Remember the difference between a syndrome and a disorder? Webster's dictionary says a syndrome is a set of concurrent things such as emotions or actions that usually form an identifiable pattern. Certain things happen in our lives and they form a pattern that is labeled a syndrome. A disorder is an abnormal physical or mental condition. If it is abnormal it is a disorder, if there is an identifiable pattern of things it becomes a syndrome. As we look at the concept of how we fight for our rights it appears to be both a syndrome and a disorder. While fighting for our rights becomes an identifiable pattern in our lives, it is also a disorder because it is not the way God wants us to think. Instead it is the way we have been taught to think. You see this especially in the United States where we have been taught and have a mindset that we have the right to have anything we want.

It is a disorder because when you go most places in the world, if you choose to do whatever you want to do and break a law of another country, you will mostly likely be thrown in jail for being a disruption to another country's government and laws. This type of activity is heard about often as Americans go to another country, do what they want, do not want to be punished by the laws of that land and then they say, "I'm an American, I have rights!" Yet just being born an American does not give people the same rights in other parts of the world. Having bought into the concept that we have rights, our emotions scream out everywhere we go that we have the right to do what we want.

Many people think they have the right to feel good. Yet one has to ask where does it say anyone has the right to feel good? They have the right to share their emotions by saying "I don't like . . . ." Bringing personal preferences and emotions into discussions, whether anyone has asked us for these or not are examples of how people push their "rights" on others. Specifically it is believed that people have the right to express when something that happens makes them angry, an emotional response to what has taken place.

People believe they have the right to express their fear. They may start a sentence with "I'm worried that . . . ," an emotional response. All these expressions, which we are taught and believe that we have the right to express are demonstrations of emotions controlling our culture. The Word of God teaches us that if we trust God we do not have to worry, we do not have to be afraid, we do not have to be angry and sometimes as difficult as this may be to read and think about, it does not matter what we like – what matters is what God wants. We dislike hearing that. We dislike knowing that because it means our emotions hold a greater say in what we do than does our God. We would rather hear that whatever we want is best while God is not as concerned with what we like as He is concerned with whether we do what He wants because we love Him so much.

We have this perception that we have the right to say how we feel. While Bonnie and I were in Wilmington, NC attempting to travel home recently, we were to be on a shuttle flight that would take us to Atlanta where we were to catch our primary flight back to Seattle. It was during bad weather conditions on the east coast which had worked its way from Florida up the eastern seafront causing many airports to shut down some of their services in and out of most airports. The flight scheduled to come and go before our flight had not even shown up. The authorities had determined the wind conditions were so bad that they did not land in North Carolina but continued down the coast to Myrtle Beach, South Carolina and chose to bus the passengers back up the coast to Wilmington. We had our seats for the next flight and were waiting for the plane to land.

This of course left the passengers that were scheduled to leave on that flight out of North Carolina stranded. There was one man in particular who was unhappy about the situation. While we were sitting about 75 feet from those standing in line this man was raking the airline counter attendant over the coals about their decision not to land. He was expressing his view that, "I am here, I have a ticket, you should have landed!" in not too nice a way. As he went on and on about his right to fly out the tension in the airport terminal began to grow with an expectation that something had to happen in response to this man's rising anger.

They were able to put him on the next flight out, which was to be our flight. Due to the shortage of seats his wife and he were able to either acquire the last two seats or were given the option to fly on the next flight out which would be Monday morning, some fifteen hours later. The attendant shared with him that other than these two options the next flight with seats available for his wife and him would be on Wednesday. Being all churned up about his circumstance he agreed to take our flight out. He sat down and the attendant continued to attempt to help the other people left from the same flight he had been scheduled on who were given very limited options. While most of the people were upset, none was as loud or obnoxious as this man.

It became apparent an hour later when no airplane had arrived at the time we were scheduled to depart that there was potential for our flight to be canceled as well. The plane we were to fly on had mechanical difficulties which kept it from taking off from Atlanta, so our flight too was canceled. The man found himself in the back of the same line with about twenty people in front of him. There was a second line next to us with an equal number of people who were waiting for assistance in determining where they would be going, how they would be getting there and where they would be spending the night as this was the last flight out of the airport until morning.

At some point the man who was previously not happy now spoke with a loud and angry tone. His first statement that roared over those in line before him was, "You lying *expletive deleted*!" He was upset. His right to fly home had been taken away from him twice now and he was taking it out verbally on the airline attendant who had already been having a difficult day due to weather conditions she could not control. She picked up a phone, made a quick call and a few moments later security showed up at the front of the line. In the mean time he was in the back of the line telling no one in particular how upset he was because he had the right to express his thoughts and his anger. His freedom of speech meant they could not arrest him; they could not do anything to him because he was angry and frustrated. As it turned out the airline drove him to another airport before he was able to fly out.

The point is that in our society we believe we have rights to do whatever we want, and we may in the sense of secular society have those rights. Yet if we are followers of Jesus Christ we have given up our rights to Jesus Christ. We no longer have the right to get angry. The point we have to realize is that when we gave our lives to Jesus Christ, we also gave Him our rights. "It is no longer I who live but Christ lives in me (Galatians 2:20)." Do you think that Jesus would be yelling and cussing because he did not get on a plane? I don't see that happening.

In this chapter you will read some concepts that might make you feel uncomfortable, particularly if you are one who is fighting for your rights. Yet when we worship our God we sing songs about personally surrendering to Him. Those are either really nice words we do not mean causing us to worship in vain or we truly mean our worship and we must change the way we think so we can be the people of God.

In our society we hold the mindset that having rights means we let our emotions control us. At the heart of the phrase "I have the right . . . ," is an emotional response to whatever it is a person wants. "Rights" are tied into our emotions and our feelings. When everything is going well with us and something happens, we do not say "I have the right . . . ." We think or say, "Its okay, let it go. It's alright." But as soon as we rise up with the "I have the right" thought, it is all about our emotions again.

There are some concepts we need to grasp to be able to change our mindset regarding our emotional response to having rights. First we need to grasp that there is a stronghold in the "I have the right" mindset. It is simply being self absorbed. It is based in "I want what I want." That is what is being said – "I want my rights." Read that phrase again putting an emphasis on each word. Two of the four words are about me. Instead of being self absorbed, we need to be like Jesus. Some people would say that this is raising the bar, yet the truth is any time I have to fight for my rights, I lower the bar. Instead of saying, "I love God and I'm going to do what He wants just like Jesus did," I am now saying, "I'm going to do what I want and fight for what I want."

Many times we have to deal with the reality that the situation we find ourselves in is not always fair. That is true, life is not always fair. My Dad and Mom used to love to tell me, "Life isn't fair." I do not know who told you life was going to be fair but God is just, and God is loving, and God is going to take care of us. Instead of getting all upset about our situation as the man did with the airline, Bonnie and I were able to step back and ask God what He had for us.

God decided to put us in a taxi to be driven two hours to Raleigh, North Carolina where He put us up in a Hilton for two nights until there was a flight available to take us home. It was not what we had in mind. Although receiving two more nights of vacation that we did not have to pay for caused us to respond with – "We're in, God!" We prayed all the way to Raleigh because it was a two hour drive in storm conditions and the driver enjoyed looking at us while he drove. Even this was a faith experience for us. We arrived in Raleigh, we stayed two nights in a Hilton Hotel which we did not have to pay for, and the airline even paid for a couple of meals. So we were grateful.

The fruit of the Spirit that comes against the My Rights Syndrome is gentleness. The biblical word for gentleness in the New Testament means strength under control. It is the word often translated meek. Meek does not mean weak, the opposite is true. The picture of meekness is a stallion that has all kinds of strength and power, yet it allows itself to be bridled and controlled by a rider, who would be Holy Spirit working through us. Gentleness comes against my rights. How many times has someone been talking about their rights and you have heard their voice get angry?

Look at 1 Samuel 25 where we will see that when some people have to fight for their rights it is a disorder. It is always an emotional response that occurs when we allow our emotions to control us, instead of controlling our emotions.

King David had been staying in Maon near a wealthy man from Carmel named Nabal was keeping his livestock. Nabal had a thousand goats and three thousand sheep. His wife, Abigail, was intelligent and beautiful yet her husband was surly and mean in his dealings. David and his men had been watching over some of Nabal's possessions while in Maon. Not one of this man's animals came up missing while David and his men were there. While in other areas raiders would come in and steal, yet because David and his six hundred men were keeping everything safe nothing from Nabal's possessions were missing.

Now the time came when Nabal's workers were going to sheer the sheep, so David sent 10 young men to share blessings (v.6) and to ask Nabal to return a blessing on David and his men by providing some food. He was expressing to Nabal, "We had six hundred hungry men and we could have feasted on your flock, taken whatever we wanted, but we did not. Instead we protected your possessions so now that it's time to shear your sheep of their wool in order to sell it for a profit, how about if you give us some food so we can share in your joyful experience by blessing us as we have blessed you."

Nabal thought about it for a little while and responded in anger because he was a surly and mean man in all his dealings. In verse 10 he said, "Who is David? And who is the son of Jesse? There are lots of servants rebelling against their masters. Should I give my bread, my water and my meat that I slaughtered for my servants and give it to a bunch of renegades?" This was not the response David was anticipating. The ten young men who were devoted to David went back and shared the response with David.

David responded by having four hundred of his men strap on their swords to go down and kill Nabal and his entire household because Nabal was not going to share with them anything after David and his men had protected them. It made sense to David and his men that after protecting someone's possessions when asked for a little bit they would at least give something to David and his men. Just in time it appeared, one of Nabal's servants went to Abigail and told her how her husband had hurled insults at David and his men. How night and day they were a "wall of protection" and he counseled her to think about what needed to be done because evil was hanging over Nabal and he was not the type of man who would listen to anybody.

Abigail, rather than tell the servant that he had no right to speak of her husband that way, realized that something bad was about to happen. Looking for a way to avoid the disaster that was hanging over her husband she had servants load up donkeys full of two hundred loaves of bread, two skins of wine, five sheep already prepared to cook and eat, five measures of roasted grain, one hundred cakes of raisins, and two hundred cakes of pressed figs. Then she took all of these provisions out to find David and his men before it was too late.

David had just gotten through saying, "Surely in vain I have guarded all that this man has in the wilderness, so that nothing was missed of all that belonged to him; and he has returned me evil for good. May God do so to the enemies of David, and more also, if by morning I leave as much as one male of any who belong to him."

You had Nabal saying "I've got nothing for you. This is my stuff and it's my right to turn you down and keep my stuff."

You had David who was saying, "I protected him, I took care of his stuff – let's go kill him. Let's go wreak vengeance on this guy!"

Then there was Abigail who came to David and immediately got off her donkey, bowed down before him and wanted David to blame her for everything. She asked him to listen to her and not pay attention to what her husband had said and done. She told David that Nabal was just like his name which meant fool, and she had not seen David's young men come and go. Then she said to David:

"Now therefore, my lord, as the LORD lives, and as your soul lives, since the LORD has restrained you from shedding blood, and from avenging yourself by your own hand" *(in Deuteronomy 32:35 the Bible says that vengeance is mine says the Lord – remember that for later)*, "now then let your enemies and those who seek evil against my lord, be as Nabal. Now let this gift which your maidservant has brought to my lord be given to the young men who accompany my lord. Please forgive the transgression of your maidservant" *(she was asking David to forgive her, not what Nabal did. She said to put the blame on her. She did not see the young men when they came for if she had this would not have happened.)* "And when the LORD does for my lord according to all the good that He has spoken concerning you, and appoints you ruler over Israel, this will not cause grief or a troubled heart to my lord, both by having shed blood without cause and by my lord having avenged himself. When the LORD deals well with my lord, then remember your maidservant."

David responded to Abigail, "Blessed be the LORD God of Israel, who sent you this day to meet me, and blessed be your discernment, and blessed be you, who have kept me this day from bloodshed and from avenging myself by my own hand. Nevertheless, as the LORD God of Israel lives, who has restrained me from harming you, unless you had come quickly to meet me, surely there would not have been left to Nabal until the morning light as much as one male." So David received from her hand what she had brought him and said to her, "Go up to your house in peace. See, I have listened to you and granted your request."

Who was right and who was wrong? Nabal's response sounded like "I have my rights, it is my stuff and I do not have to give you anything." Yet David had done so much for him one would think he would want to bless David. Nabal was wrong for his emotional response of anger and the surly attitude he had.

David's attitude sounded like, "Since I protected you and you have done nothing in return, I am going to take vengeance out on you." David was wrong because he took the position that it was his right to get paid for something he chose to do without being asked. If it was done out of the kindness of his heart then he should have expected nothing in return. He had not entered into a contract with Nabal. He had no agreement with Nabal. He had assumed because he and his men had done nice things for Nabal that Nabal would do something for him in return. David was wrong because his emotional response was in anger he was going to take vengeance out on this man and his household because he thought he had the right to be taken care of for his kindness. Interesting thought, had God told David to take vengeance out on Nabal?

The only person in this account who did the right thing was Abigail. She stepped into the middle of the fight between these two emotional men and appealed to David not to follow through on his angry thoughts and statements. She soothed David's temper by offering him gifts. She saved David from shedding blood, and he had agreed he would have hated himself for it later on in life.

She had said to him, "And when the LORD does for my lord according to all the good that He has spoken concerning you, and appoints you ruler over Israel, this will not cause grief or a troubled heart to my lord, both by having shed blood without cause and by my lord having avenged himself. When the LORD deals well with my lord, then remember your maidservant."

The NIV puts it this way "my master will not have on his conscience the staggering burden of needless bloodshed . . . ." The staggering burden of needless bloodshed just for a few sheep and goats. This is David, the man after God's own heart, fighting for his rights. God allows this woman to step in and say "Don't do it!" and David listened to her. Right now there is a thought running through a lot of women's minds – "If they would listen to us there would be a lot of things that would not go the wrong way." Men, that thought may be correct. Yet if you are more concerned about your right to make decisions without her input, you will never agree. In this case it was true.

Next Abigail went back to her husband and to tell him everything she had done. Nabal had been out partying at his own banquet, had become drunk on his wine and in the morning when he was no longer drunk but probably had quite the hangover, she told him these things and then his heart, the Bible said, "died within him and became as a stone" and ten days later the Lord struck him dead. Vengeance is mine says the Lord.

David did not end up carrying bloodshed, the staggering burden of having done something God did not want him to do. Even though his emotions had risen up and deceived him into thinking what he was about to do was his right and the correct thing to do. David was wrong to think he was correct to be angry about something like this. Yet God took care of the situation.

Nabal's response was "My right, my stuff and my anger." He was totally self absorbed. David's response was "My honor, my rights, my rage," and he was totally self absorbed. But Abigail's response was "Your honor, your dignity, my responsibility." She was meek and she was gentle. Her example is how we are supposed to respond to the issue of rights. We have to understand that it is not about my rights but about doing what is right.

In life if we are followers of Jesus Christ it is not about our rights but about doing what is right. This entire syndrome ties into the "Nobody can tell me what to do mindset," because I have rights. Nobody can tell me what to do is an emotional response. While watching an interview of a rookie quarterback in the NFL once I heard him say "Nobody can tell me what to do." How wrong is that thought? Implied in that is "I'll do whatever I want." No, he will do what the coach tells him to do or he will sit on the bench. People have this mindset and it is based on a misunderstanding of submission and not being willing to trust God.

When someone says, "Nobody can tell me what to do," they are saying, "I do not trust God so I need to handle this myself." Submission is choosing to align with someone else. It is a choice everybody has to make. It is always easy to agree with someone when they think the way you do, but as soon as someone thinks differently than we do, that is when submission is actually tested. That is when we find out if we are going to choose to stay aligned with another person. Even if I were to go to an individual and say "I do not agree with the direction you are going, I think we should do this instead." When the person says "This is the direction we are going anyway" what do I do, stay aligned with them, or walk away?

When at work and the boss says "This is what you are going to do."

You do it if you want to keep your job. Suppose you say "I think there is an easier way to answer the phone and pass on messages at work."

If the boss says, "That's not how I want you to do it."

And you respond with "I'm sure there is an easier way."

The boss tells you, "It does not matter this is how I want you to do it."

You submit to their way and align with that person ultimately saying, "If that's how you want me to do it, you are paying me, I will do it the way you want me to do it."

If you do not do it the way the boss wants you to do it, inevitably what will happen? You will get fired.

I want to be like Jesus in everything. I want to be like Jesus with signs, wonders and miracles and healings. I want to be like Jesus in everything. In John 12:27-28 after Jesus predicted His death he said, "Now My soul has become troubled; and what shall I say, 'Father, save Me from this hour'? But for this purpose I came to this hour." Instead of saying "Father save Me from this, Father don't let this happen to Me. Jesus said, "Father, glorify Your name." Did you notice that Jesus' emotions had been stirring in Him? His soul was troubled. He did not want to go through the crucifixion. Yet He did not give in to His emotions, He controlled them in order to accomplish what Father God had sent Him to do.

In Matthew 26 just prior to the trials and crucifixion of Jesus, He had already asked the disciples to stay awake and pray with Him because His soul was so overwhelmed with the emotion of sorrow, even sorrow to the point of death. While on His face talking with Father God Jesus said, "My Father, if it is possible, let this cup pass from Me. (That's a real nice way of saying "I don't want to do this!") Then Jesus said, "Yet not as I will, but as You will." He is telling Father God "Whatever you want."

Then He had gone away a second time after finding His disciples all asleep when he had asked them to stay awake and pray. Rather than getting mad at them in the midst of being rocked emotionally due to the fact that He knew He was about to go through this incredible torture and die, He woke them up and asked them why they were not able to be praying with Him for one hour. He told them to watch and pray so they would not fall into temptation for their spirit was willing but their flesh was what was weak. Jesus went back to His conversation with Father God and said the same thing again, that if this cup could not be taken away from Him unless this was how God's will would be done, Jesus was willing to do it.

Do you see that more than once Jesus told Father God He did not want to go through it, He did not want to suffer like He knew He was going to have to suffer? Jesus told Father God that if this was the only way that Father's will could be done, then if it glorified Father God He would do it. That is submission. Rather than being in a situation where I am arguing with a human being whether to align and be submissive to that person, what needs to be done is what Jesus did which is to fall in line and say: "I may not want to do this Lord, but if this is what I am supposed to do then I am going to do it. If this is why you have put me here then I am going to fall into line and do these things the way that I am being asked or told to do them." If you think the difference is between being asked or told to do something you have missed the point. Submission is aligning myself and agreeing to do what I have been asked or told to do.

We need to understand that it is all about trusting God and not about trusting other people. We think that submission and authority is about trusting other people, but it is all about trusting God. If one is not able to trust God then they will not be able to trust others to do what they are supposed to do. If I cannot trust God then when the Elders tell me, "We think we should do this," then I will not trust them. If you are unable to trust God, then in any relationship you have, when someone has asked you to do something in authority or in any relationship, you will have trouble trusting them.

Expect it to start with suspicion. Suspicion will come into your heart and your mind and you will start to think there must be something wrong here. As you begin to think about that other thoughts will come to your mind that will cause you to doubt whether you should align yourself while trusting God that you are able to do what He wants. Those thoughts will challenge you and push you down a road that will drive you away from doing what God wants and lead you to a point of making a decision which God does not want you to make. If you are trusting God, any time suspicion is put in your mind you will stop and ask God whether those thoughts are from Him. If you cannot trust God you will not be able to submit to people. All through life there will be people over and around us that we will need to submit to.

When you step back and think about it, your struggle is less with the person telling you what to do and more with trusting God that He is able to protect you, lead you, care for you, and give you the strength and wisdom to do what He wants you to do. This all comes out of a covenant relationship with God. When someone tells God, "I give you my life," at that point there is an entering into a covenant with God whereby declaring He is the Lord of that person's life. They have given to God their rights, their ambitions, their hopes, their plans; they have given all of their life to Him and they are going to do whatever it is that God has for them to do. If they are going to go down a road where there is the possibility of making $40 million and God says, "Not anymore, I want you to do something else instead that will not pay nearly as well", then the person who has given their life to God says, "Whatever you want me to do." There may be a great struggle that takes place at that point, even as there was with Jesus, but ultimately the person will say to God, "Whatever you want."

The other side of this thought is that if you are doing what God has told you and He decides it is time to shift you over to another assignment where you will be making $40 million in the next five years because He wants you to have the funding available so His Kingdom advances, then shift into that. Whatever it is He has given us to do we should be able to thank Him. The problem comes when He shifts us to a different assignment and we no longer trust Him with what He has given us because we want something else. Instead of saying, "God you've given me a car, you've given me a job or you've given me all these things and I am going to keep walking with you," we start pulling back from our relationship with God and we say, "I have all these things and I have to figure out a way to keep them." We then step out from aligning with God and we do what we want to do.

People tend to turn leadership and submission into a "my rights" issue. I have rights, so I do not have to follow leaders, even God ordained leaders. I do not have to submit unless I want to because I have rights, too. Eph 5:21 speaks about believers being willing to submit to one another in the fear of Christ. But so many people say to leaders, "I have the right to be equal with you when it comes to decisions," and are equally unwilling to submit to one another by honoring one another as more important than themselves (Romans 12:10). There is an attitude that implies and often says, "We could be doing it better if you would do it my way instead of following you and God."

It is a covenantal relationship issue where rather than stay in covenant with each other by saying, "We have made an agreement to follow you because God has told us to follow our leaders and learn from each other," the opposite occurs, war breaks loose in the camp and people start demanding their rights which they have given to God along with the rest of their lives.

What we need to do is extend grace and mercy rather than fight for our rights. When Jesus is our Lord we need to extend grace and mercy to others. When Jesus is our Lord He is supposed to be master of our emotions and our rights. Because of our covenant relationship our relationships with each other are a picture of our relationship with God. If we are in covenant with God, we are in covenant with each other. If we are at war with each other, the one who does not want peace with other members of God's family is at war with God. When a person starts to argue for their rights they have just told God, "I'll take care of this. I have it under control. Give me back my rights I have told you belong to you."

At that point God often watches as you step away from Him and He says to you, "Your emotions have run amok. You are allowing them to color what you are thinking instead of trusting Me even though you think you have it under control." Then if we continue not to listen we fire off an email to get our point across and deal with an issue we should leave in His hands. We call a person or sit down with a person often outside the timing of God while Holy Spirit is telling us not to do that.

1 Corinthians 6:7 says, "Why not rather be wronged? Why not rather be defrauded?" In a teaching about Christians going to court against each other Paul asks us why not rather be wronged? That question flies in the face of the person who thinks they need to cry out for their rights. Why not rather be wronged rather than fight for what you think is your right? In 1 Samuel 24:12 David basically says "Let it go, you don't have to fight for it, let it go."

Over and over when sharing counsel with individuals who get into arguments with each other, we say the best way to end an argument is to let it go. We have to understand and put into practice this simple thought: "I don't have to be right; I don't have to get my way". Rather than say that one last point that you are sure is going to clarify everything for the person you are arguing with, let it go. You do not have to fight for your rights, God knows your rights. He is going to take care of you. He is going to bless you. He is going to do for you everything that is good, because God is good. Every good gift comes down from God. We just have to trust Him and realize it is okay if I let it go because God is going to make it right in the long run. It is okay to let it go because I want to be like Jesus. In Philippians chapter two it is clear what we can do to be like Jesus.

The Bible says, "Your attitude should be the same as that of Christ Jesus: Who, being in very nature God, did not consider equality with God something to be grasped." Even though the Son of God could have said "I don't want to go down and live with those people." He knew that rather than hold on to equality with God He could come to earth and by doing so, let go of it. He did not have to hold on to His rights. Even on earth he did not demand the right of people to respect and honor Him – He let go of that right.

The Bible goes on to say, "Jesus made himself nothing, taking the very nature of a servant, being made in human like-ness. And being found in appearance as a man, he humbled himself and became obedient to death – even death on a cross!" He gave up His rights. He did not even fight for His rights. He did not say, "This is not right!" When Peter pulled a sword in the garden of Gethsemane and cut off a man's ear after picking up the ear and healing it Jesus told him, "Do you think I cannot call on my Father, and he will at once put at my disposal more than twelve legions of angels?" NIV

Jesus could have done that, but it was not why He was here. He had the authority and power to wipe out those who were abusing His rights, but Jesus said, "No, I'm going to trust Father God."

And Philippians 2:9-11 tell us Father God blessed Him for His obedience and because He did it God's way, "God exalted him to the highest place and gave him the name that is above every name, that at the name of Jesus every knee should bow, in heaven and on earth and under the earth, and every tongue confess that Jesus Christ is Lord, to the glory of God the Father." NIV

Do you want to be like Jesus? Then you should not fight for your rights. Even though in America we have our rights, we should not have to fight for them. If we go to prayer we will either be told by God not to worry about our rights or we will be told by God He is going to take care of the situation, and you will be blessed because you did what Jesus did.

At that point it is our choice what we are going to do. Are we going to fight for our rights or do what God wants us to do by trusting Him? The sooner we realize that fighting for our rights is about our emotions overcoming what the Spirit of God wants, the sooner we will change the way we think and we will begin to walk in the Spirit. God will bless us for it in incredible ways. If there are rights you have been holding onto, hopes and dreams that you have been unwilling to give to God, take some time to release them to God now and begin the journey of peace that comes from not having to stand up for or fight for your rights. Give these things to God again if you have already given them to Him before. If you keep giving them to Him, eventually you will stop taking them back.

Tell Him you don't want to go back to your old life. You want to be who God says you are. You want to see yourself the way God sees you, a person who wants to be like Jesus who gave up His rights. When you see someone else fighting for their rights, would you ask God to bless them with peace? If you have already surrendered your rights to God, then thank Him for taking them and for setting you free from the Syndrome and Disorder of having to fight for your rights, because while you allow God to hold your rights, He is saying well done good and faithful servant.

## Chapter 8

# The "Justification" Syndrome

S hortly before a recent election I was asked by the mayor of a city to be the moderator of a town hall meeting for the candidates running for office in that city. After checking with our Elders, Church Officers and my wife and being encouraged by them to be the moderator I was honored to take on this responsibility. Four of the candidates chose not to show up. About two thirds of the way through the meeting a younger woman stood and said, "I thought I was coming to a debate between all the candidates." I had to tell everyone present that "For one reason or another some of the candidates chose not to show up."

It would have been easy to justify why they were not present to discuss their views on a variety of topics. "People have busy schedules and I'm sure they were just too busy to come." There were any number of ways that their absences could have been justified, but the best explanation without justifying was what was shared. That is what should be done more often, speak the truth in love and not add to it.

When a person justifies their actions they are declaring themselves not guilty of wrong doing. By justifying themselves they try to show that they are just, right, or proper about what they have done. They try to declare themselves guiltless or blameless. They try to show sufficient reason for something having happened, particularly something that was done.

Sometimes this can be heard in statements like "he made me do it." "You made me throw my mashed potatoes across the table and hit you in the face." A justification of what has been done does not usually work well, but people try to do it. Even when a person is right and they try to justify it, others will often step back and say, "I don't know . . . ."

This Syndrome can be heard in statements like: "I couldn't help myself," "I was so angry the words just came out," "I was so jealous." Some people justify actions by saying "It's okay to feel that way because . . . ." These are all ways people justify their words and actions. If we are honest, we have all done this at some time. Yet it is seen more and more. Rather than people stepping up and saying "I did this and it was wrong," there are all kinds of ways to put a spin on what is done. "It wasn't really my fault." Have you ever heard someone say that? Perhaps you have at least thought it? Usually it is a phrase that comes out when someone feels guilty about what they did or said, or when confronted with improper behavior.

"I was raised that way," "I was born that way," or "Somebody did this to me." When someone tries to justify what they have done they are allowing their emotions to control what they do. Rather than say, "I didn't clean the kitchen when I said I would" often a phrase trying to justify our wrong doing is added like "It was not my fault though, I was answering email." That type of explanation is not taking responsibility for what was not done. When someone says, "I would have done it but . . . ." or "I was watching football and just got caught up in the game."

What needs to be said is "I didn't get it done because I allowed my emotions to pull me in a direction different than what I said I would do." Instead we tend to use an emotion filled reason for not doing something that was important to the other person.

We justify our words. We justify our actions. We justify our thinking, even our emotions at times. We choose not to take responsibility for our own emotional responses that are being displayed by our own words, actions and reactions. Everyone sees this type of behavior, even when it is not you personally. It can be seen every day.

Professional athletes attempt to justify what they have done. There are people in politics that get caught doing something wrong and they attempt to justify it. This type of explanation for an action is seen in every area of life.

In the story of Nabal and David looked at in the previous chapter, one can imagine both men justifying what they said or did. Nabal may have said, "David did nothing for me." In 1 Samuel 25 he asked "Who is he anyway, that he would say I owe him food?" He was justifying his decision to treat David and his men unkindly. David justified why he was going to go kill Nabal's entire household. "How dare he do this, this is an issue of honor. I have the right to do these things." He was justifying why he was about to kill people.

It is a stronghold of pride, insecurity or irresponsibility that causes people to react in this manner. Yet often in our culture if someone steps up and admits they have done something improper, takes responsibility for it being wrong and asks forgiveness, most of the time people are willing to forgive or at least let it go. There may still be consequences depending on the severity of the impropriety, but it is proven to be better to step up and admit they did it.

We have been taught since we were little it is the correct action to take. Remember the story of George Washington as it has been told for decades? He chopped down the cherry tree and what did he do? Did he make excuses for it? No, he told his father he chopped down the cherry tree. This story is an attempt to teach each other not to justify what has gone on in our lives, in our country, or in our city. We need to learn to speak what happened without excuse.

People become caught up in justifying their emotional reaction and an identifiable pattern in their lives becomes evident. After the second or third time a child begins this behavior of making excuses for themselves it becomes easier to see. If as an employer or supervisor the employees who work under you start making excuses for why they have not done something in order to justify their action or inaction, are you able to recognize that? If a student comes to class who has forgotten to bring their homework with them and they have any number of excuses doesn't the teacher watch them to see if this is a recurring pattern?

There are two types of people who justify their actions. First of all there are those who have yet to give their lives to Jesus and who justify their actions. Then there are the followers of Jesus Christ who justify their actions. Let's look at how the Justification Syndrome affects the second group; those who are believers in Jesus Christ. They may be heard saying, "It's okay that I choose to do this over what God has for me." There are people who have given their lives to Jesus, who justify why they do not follow Him. Followers of Jesus Christ are people who want to be like Jesus.

In Acts 15 there is an example of this. Paul and Barnabas had returned to Jerusalem and had shared all the incredible things that God had done. The miracles, the signs and wonders, and the whole assembly had become silent as they listened to them share so much of what God had done through them. Then in verse 36 Paul suggested to Barnabas that they go back and visit again all the believers in all the towns and see how they were doing. Barnabas thought it was a great idea and wanted to take John Mark along with them. Paul responded with "I don't think so. He left in the middle of our last trip and I don't think we should take him."

Barnabas suggested that it would be a good thing to encourage the young man. The conversation must have continued in this type of manner because they had such a sharp disagreement they parted company. These were two apostles, two men of God. They were involved in such a strong an argument that they decided not to travel together anymore causing them to go two different directions. How did they justify that? Paul justified it with the perspective that because John Mark left last time, he could not be trusted to finish the trip a second time. Barnabas justified it with the perspective that it didn't matter what Paul thought, with some encouragement John Mark could be a great asset. Either way, they allowed their emotions to control their decision of no longer ministering together, justifying their decisions even though God had done such amazing things through them on their first trip.

Who was wrong? Was it Paul or Barnabas? The Bible never says if one of them or both of them were wrong. Some people would say it must have been Barnabas because he was not heard of again in the book of Acts. Yet three times in the epistles Paul mentions Mark and in Second Timothy he told Timothy to send Mark because he was useful now. Is that strange? It appears Barnabas takes John Mark, mentors him, and trains him up to be an effective minister because he showed mercy to John Mark. Yet years later Paul recognized that he had become the man of God he needed to be to help in the ministry. Is it possible that although they were in sharp disagreement, they both could have been hearing from God? Barnabas was suppose to take Mark and train him up, Paul knew that he was supposed to go do other things and Mark was not ready to go. It became a disagreement because their emotions took over when mercy was needed to be displayed. And they justified themselves in the process. When they could have parted company according to God's will and blessed each other as they went different directions.

Does that mean apostles made mistakes? Yes, of course they did. They do today. In Galatians Paul confronted Peter about a mistake he was making. There will be times when we need to say "This is what God wants me to do." Only time will demonstrate whether it was the Lord's leading, depending on the fruit of the person's ministry and life. If you have wondered whether someone else's decision to do something was of God, only time will tell. Yet in their going it would be good to say "God bless you as you follow Him." Put your blessing on them then let them go. Do not justify why you are upset or may disagree with them. The truth be told you might be upset because you do not want them to go do what it is they believe they should be doing. You may want them to stay with you. Even when you are wondering how they can justify their decision. I believe the Lord wants us to show mercy to people.

The way to overcome the justification syndrome is to stop justifying what we do and be like Jesus. If there is an issue of sin, just admit it rather than trying to cover it with a reason for having done it. If you were supposed to do one thing at home, work, school or ministry and you did not do it, go to the person and say to them, "I was supposed to do this and I did not do it. I was wrong." Just admit it. The sooner one person admits there is something wrong, the sooner the relationship may be restored. As long as people stay in this tug of war about who was right and who was wrong then it has to be asked what is actually being accomplished for God's Kingdom? We need to restore people who are caught up in sin, who fall into it, or who are involved in it. We do not need to excuse it or justify it. People need to be loved and restored.

In 2 Corinthians the Bible tells us that we have been called to a ministry of reconciliation. In Norm Willis' book <u>Unity With A Return</u> on pages 91-94 he shares five distinct tactics of thiefology to bring people to the point of not trusting others.

First he shares there is a seed of suspicion that is planted. Someone may say something that causes you to question someone else. It is just a seed of suspicion. "I don't know about Mary, she used to sit over here, but now she is sitting over there." Just that seed makes you begin to wonder why Mary is not sitting over here anymore. That is how quickly the door of accusation opens. "Why do you think . . .?" is asked, allowing suspicion to lead to an accusation. "Clearly she is not sitting there anymore because something must have been said." There is a wrongful presupposition that is developed before anything ever happens. The suspicion was made into an accusation bringing the presupposition of "therefore, this is what happened. This must be why."

We have no idea why, it may be that Mary has chosen to sit in a different place this week because she wants to. While there is nothing wrong with her choosing to sit somewhere different when there is a pattern of suspicion which leads to accusation based on a wrongful presupposition we draw faulty conclusions about people. "Mary must be out of favor with God because she won't sit over there where she used to sit." If left alone with suspicion and accusation long enough it is easy to come up with all kinds of whacked out ideas.

A husband may begin to wonder why his wife is late coming home from work. A seed of suspicion enters in leading to an accusation based on a wrongful presupposition drawing a faulty conclusion – "I'll bet she took the car out four wheeling." We laugh at such a preposterous thought yet it is as ridiculous as some of the other thoughts we come up with when we start down this road based on the tactics of the enemy of our soul. For as soon as the seed of accusation is allowed to be planted we allow it to run wild in our thoughts. That decision leads us to a wrongful conclusion which usually all takes place in isolation. You see if we were talking to mature and godly individuals they would point out the fallacy of that thinking. But when we get isolated, are alone or with a couple of other people, and some sort of miscommunication takes place we make decisions based on a suspicion that led us down this road. This happens all too frequently. Then we have to justify why we came to that conclusion.

Having given some thought to this, watch this week for seeds of suspicion that could become planted. These seeds may be spread by someone at work, by a family member who brings up another person that invokes a mental reaction accusing them of having an attitude that has not been displayed before. Be aware of this process and do not justify suspicion in your life. Keep from justifying accusations in your life. Stop from thinking because they have done one thing in the past therefore it is okay to justify thinking a certain way about them in the present. Determine you are not going to go there mentally.

If you are wondering what is wrong with heading down this road mentally, ponder it from a personal perspective. Would it not bother you if someone was suspicious of you? Of course it would, so we need to keep from doing this to others. Why?

We want to be like Jesus. Jesus kept from justifying anything He did. When He was brought before Pontius Pilate and the religious leaders at the mock trials that were held, Jesus did not answer them. He chose to be silent rather than justify what He had done. During His life He was asked by what authority He healed people. He responded by agreeing to answer their question if they first would answer His question. After asking His question about where John the Baptist received his authority, the religious leaders stepped back, put their collective heads together. They realized if they said it was God, then Jesus would have asked them why they didn't believe him. But if they said his authority came from men, they were afraid of the people who thought John was a prophet. So the leaders came back and told Jesus they did not know. So Jesus would not answer their question either. Learning from Jesus people do not have to justify what they do.

I learned a personal lesson when one Fall someone sent a two page letter single spaced wanting me to explain why I was not involved in the political process like the writer of the letter thought pastors should by telling their local congregations how to vote and marching against certain issues. It was a long letter chewing me out because of the author's perception of reality. I have learned that perception does not become reality, perception instead distorts reality. Sitting down that morning I decided to answer the questions and respond to the perceptions. After spending about three hours writing, rewriting and editing my responses I had concisely answered every one of the questions posed. Then I took it into a friend of mine Brad Barshaw who was our District Superintendent and asked him what he thought of it.

After reading the man's letter and reading my letter of response he said, "Let me ask you a question. Do you want to continue these discussions with this man?"

I said: "No, I am hoping this letter puts it to rest."

Brad said something like: "It's not going to because you have just given him plenty of ammunition to ask more questions." What he was teaching me was to stop justifying my lack of involvement with political issues. "If I were you," he said, "I'd send him a letter that simply acknowledges that you have received his letter, you understand what he is saying, and you hope and pray that God blesses him as he pursues God in the political process. Then sign your name."

After his sage advice I realized that I had flushed away three hours of my day. In choosing to send a letter of three sentences that did not justify my actions, I did not hear from the man again. While it appeared he was looking to pick a fight with me over his political agenda, I learned not to engage with someone just because they want to argue. There are better ways to spend our time. If someone asks a question looking for an answer that will help them, then answering a question is a good move. But when someone keeps coming with more and more questions there is a deeper issue. They have received the seed of suspicion. The door of accusation which was opened has been walked through by them. They already have some presuppositions and conclusions which they are getting ready to use to make a decision. It will not matter what I say to them, they have already made the decision which will be clouded by thoughts they will usually not even make me aware of.

Rather than spend hours in the midst of fruitless justification of why we do what we do, it is better to send a note that expresses a desire for them to get the answers God wants them to have as they pursue God and let it go. If we want to be like Jesus, we do not have to justify what we do.

In Matthew 9:9-13 Jesus walked up to Matthew who was a tax collector and said two words: "Follow Me." Matthew responded by getting up and following Jesus because Matthew, like so many people today, must have been looking for someone, or something to follow. He would not have just walked away from everything if there was not a reason to walk away. He must have been looking for Jesus to follow and all around us today there are people who are looking for Jesus, wanting to experience Him and follow Him. We only need to invite them to come join God in what He is doing. They will come check it out.

Matthew invited his friends and Jesus to his house for a dinner party. He invited tax collectors and others who most of the people of his time disliked and called "sinners." In The Phillips Translation, J. B. Phillips used the phrase "disreputable people" instead of "sinners" (p. 18). These were people the religious leaders and many others looked down on. These people all show up at this party where Jesus and the others were and had a good enough time that it bugged the religious leaders. They pulled aside Jesus' disciples because rather than talk with Jesus they wanted to plant the seed of suspicion with the ones who were committed followers of Jesus.

They did this by asking why their teacher ate with tax collectors and sinners. Why He even hung out with these people? Jesus told them, "It's not the healthy that need a doctor, but the sick." Then He made their problem obvious to those who had ears to hear. Jesus quotes from Hosea 6:6 where God said "I desire mercy not sacrifice." He told them He had not come to call the righteous but sinners.

When people justify when they do something wrong, we need to show mercy to bring them back to Jesus. Mercy is not saying it is okay for people to do whatever they want to do. We need to show mercy and compassion by loving people and helping them to understand why they did what they did rather than justify their actions. Get past all that is being said, ask God why they did what they did, what is at the heart of their actions in order to demonstrate mercy and God's love to them. God's mercy and love is what people are missing in their lives.

Many people today are wondering how to do that. It is a great question that Jesus answered in Luke 6:27-36. Jesus shared 10 commands that we are to do even today which are followed by two statements that tell us what the result of our obeying Jesus' commands will be. Jesus said: "But I say to you who hear. . . ." He started by saying listen up. Jesus brought up in Matthew, Mark and Luke that anyone who has ears to hear should listen up.

Then Jesus said to "love your enemies." This is a choice we have to make. While love seems to be so much about emotion today, it is actually about choosing. Love is an act of self sacrifice for the good of another person. We choose to love other people. To understand how to love others, let's look at 1 Corinthians 13 where how to love people is explained. 1 Corinthians 13 says, "Love is patient." So if we are going to love our enemies we need to be patient with them. "Love is kind" which means to love one's enemies we need to look for a way of being constructive in their lives. "It is not jealous; love does not brag and is not arrogant, does not act unbecomingly; it does not seek its own, is not provoked, does not take into account a wrong suffered, does not rejoice in unrighteousness, but rejoices with the truth; bears all things, believes all things, hopes all things, endures all things. Love never fails."

The phrase "love never fails" is a picture of a building that carries the idea it will never fall down. It has been built in such a way that it will continue to stand. That is what love is supposed to be as we display it to each other, even to our enemies. In loving people we never intentionally hurt them.

Jesus went on in Luke 6 to say: "do good to those who hate you." Have you thought about doing good to those who hate you? Even if they try to justify why they hate you? You are still supposed to do good to them.

He said, "Bless those who curse you." So many want to hold onto what God told Abraham in the Old Testament. God told him He would bless those who blessed Him and curse those who cursed Him, but Jesus lifts us to a higher standard by telling His followers to bless those who curse us. Even when someone drives by on the freeway and waves at you with one finger, bless them. Say out loud to them "God bless you."

Then Jesus said: "pray for those who mistreat you." The word mistreat means they insult you or use you spitefully, they use you with extreme hatred and spite. These are people who really do not like you and you probably know it. Jesus says pray for them. Love them, do good things for them, bless them and pray for them. If you are loving people, you will do good things for them, and bless them; when we pray for them we are praying good things into their lives. You may ask God to bring people into their lives who will influence them to want to be like Jesus.

Next Jesus said, "Whoever hits you on the cheek, offer him the other also." What He was saying is do not fight with them. Turn and walk away if you have to but do not fight with them. After studying through the Sermon on the Mount years ago there were two or three parents who came and said, "I know that is what Jesus said but I'm teaching my kid to swing back." When we know what Jesus said and get upset anyway we need to admit that we are upset at God and most people do not want to think they are angry with God. It is easier to be mad at somebody else. Jesus said to turn the other cheek. When they slap you, love them, do good for them, bless them and pray for them. The thought may come to mind, "But they just hit me!" Jesus said to turn the other cheek.

"Whoever takes away your coat, do not withhold your shirt from him either." If you have a coat on and they take it, offer them your shirt as well. People think that is ridiculous but in Jesus' day Roman soldiers could walk up and take their cloak from them. Jesus was saying to give them your shirt as well. It may not seem like it makes sense, but from God's perspective it displays mercy to the person.

Then Jesus went radical. He told them to give to everyone who asked of them, and whoever took away what was theirs, they were not demand it back. For us it means if someone borrows a book, a DVD, or a tool, Jesus said "Don't demand it back."

If you are thinking, "What? That makes no sense."

I know, yet Jesus said that so it made sense to Him. Look in your Bible – in verse thirty does He say something like "Don't demand it back?"

In verse thirty one Jesus added: "Treat others the same way you want them to treat you." That is the golden rule. Do to others as you would have them do to you. So we should be loving everybody, blessing everybody, doing good to every-body, praying for everybody and not caring about when they justify what they did. Is that even possible? That's what Jesus said to do. That's what is at the heart of this. We can deal with our own justifying of what we do. We can sit down with people and help them understand they are justifying their actions, but Jesus was saying whether they understand it or not we are to keep on loving them.

"If you love those who love you, what credit is that to you? For even sinners love those who love them. If you do good to those who do good to you, what credit is that to you? For even sinners do the same. If you lend to those from whom you expect to receive, what credit is that to you? Even sinners lend to sinners in order to receive back the same amount. But love your enemies, and do good, and lend, expecting nothing in return; and your reward will be great, and you will be sons of the Most High; for He Himself is kind to ungrateful and evil men. Be merciful, just as your Father is merciful."

It is easy to love those who love us. It is easy to do good to those who do good to us. It is easy to lend to people we expect to receive back from. Yet Jesus is saying to us today "Love those who don't love you back. Lend to those who will not return what you have lent to them. Do good to them and lend. Do not expect anything in return and then, yes then your reward will be great.

Does this passage make you uncomfortable? Look at the end result. After living lives like this, our reward will be great and we will be children of the Most High. We will be merciful as Father God is merciful. We are supposed to do this because God Himself is kind to ungrateful and evil people. Think for a minute about that. Does God love His enemies? Yes, He loved us even when we were still sinners and ignored Him. Did God do good to us even before we gave our lives to Him, when we chose not to follow Him? Yes! Did God bless us even when we may have cursed Him?

Does Jesus intercede for us even though we mistreat Him or do not do what He wants? Yes!

When Jesus was struck on one cheek did He turn the other cheek? Did He give up everything, even His clothes which they gambled over at the cross? Did Jesus give to everyone who asked Him? Did He heal people no matter the time of day or night? And He fed thousands, not expecting anything in return. Did Jesus ever demand things back from people? Do you want to be like Jesus?

What makes these commands hard is that this is what Jesus did. Do we want to be like Jesus in everything or just when it is comfortable? If we do to others as we want them to do to us we will be nice to people even if they are not nice to us. It is the spiritual law of reaping what we have sown. So if you are out being good to people and blessing people, people will be good to you and bless you. Is that what you want?

If you are out putting curses on people, yelling at people and treating them poorly – no matter how much you think you can justify it, you should expect that you are going to have people cursing you, yelling at you and treating you poorly. Because what you sow you will reap. So from a logical perspective it makes sense to obey what Jesus has said. The result of being like Jesus is there will be a reward waiting for us in heaven, and we will be rewarded in this lifetime.

In Mark 10:28 Jesus was in a discussion with His disciples and He made this very point about being rewarded in this lifetime. Peter began to say to Him, "Behold, we have left everything and followed You." Jesus said, "Truly I say to you, there is no one who has left house or brothers or sisters or mother or father or children or farms, for My sake and for the gospel's sake, but that he will receive a hundred times as much now *in the present age*, houses and brothers and sisters and mothers and children and farms, along with persecutions; and in the age to come, eternal life. But many who are first will be last, and the last, first." (Italics added.)

He mentioned persecutions will come with this. But the point is whatever you give up for God He will bless you with more of. When someone comes to borrow something from you, you can loan it to them with great joy because you know God will bless you with more than what you just gave. How do you know that? Because Jesus said that and He does not lie.

There is no need for us to justify why we do what we do. Remember, we defined justifying as an emotional response by declaring oneself not guilty of wrong doing. By justifying oneself they try to show that they are just, right, or proper about what they have done. Yet this justifying is most often displayed when trying to clear one's name from not doing what God wants, or not being like Jesus. If we are treating people with this kind of love, we will never need to justify what we do. So rather than justifying what we do, let's live a life that does not require justifying. Let's live the life that Jesus said to live. Let's look for people to be good to. Let somebody else have that parking space at the mall. Who would come up to you and ask "Why did you love him? Why did you do that nice thing to that person?" If they cannot understand why you would demonstrate that kind of love they leave the door wide open for you to say, "Because Jesus did. Cause I want to be like Jesus. And you can be like Jesus too."

## Chapter 9

# The "Righteous Indignation" Syndrome

A lady was telling me about a letter printed in the New York
Times on July 29, 2007, by thirty evangelical leaders
who held a position different than hers. She was worked up
about it. The letter in essence told then President Bush that
there were large numbers of Evangelicals who supported not
only justice for both the Israelis and the Palestinians, but
also wanted to encourage the President to move ahead with
a two state solution which included dividing Jerusalem as
part of the answer.

The lady who shared this with me was "indignant." For
most people in evangelical churches there is little concern
about this issue. Yet for her this was a huge issue. She would
have said that she was "righteously indignant" about the fact
that America's leaders were talking about dividing Israel and
Jerusalem. She made this comment. "I don't understand how
intelligent, Spirit-filled people could think this way." She
was very upset. My response was in the form of a question.
"We believe a lot of things have to fall in place for Jesus to
return, what if they do not want Jesus to return yet so they
are saying 'Divide Israel up?' What if they have a thought

behind what they are doing that is different than what you want?"

There is this word in the New Testament we see a handful of times – the word indignation. It means "strong displeasure at something considered unjust, something offensive, or insulting." Since the Ephesians 4:22 tells us to be angry and yet do not sin, there evidently is a way to be angry without it leading us to sin. The issue is not that one becomes angry, it is what they do with the anger that opens the door to sin. Most of the time people become angry they say something like, "I have a right to be angry." Some will call it righteous indignation. This usually means the person is trying to justify their emotion.

It seems that most of the time when people are upset at someone else and become indignant with others it is because they are upset at themselves for not having done what God wanted them to do. Most people become indignant because they have either anger issues or are unwilling to forgive. It is easier to point a finger at someone else for what they have not done because it emotionally makes the person feel better.

The Righteous Indignation Syndrome can be claimed and seen when people are yelling, screaming or carrying banners about any number of topics. It can be seen when people argue over doctrinal differences, and there is a difference between arguing and discussing. Most of the time people may discuss something but when anger comes into the discussion, it becomes an argument dividing the Church of Jesus Christ against itself.

We see the Righteous Indignation Syndrome being justified and demonstrated in the issue of how people prefer to worship and the expressions of their worship. There was a time a few years ago at a Pastors and Wives Retreat my wife and I attended where there was a heated discussion (heated discussions means an argument broke out) that took place over a lunch table about the proper use of hymns in worship.

Rather than seeing it as a matter of personal preference, which styles of worship are about, this discussion turned quickly into an argument as people justified their preference of worship music in angry ways. To disagree with each other allowed their righteous indignation to arise and disrupt the relationships forming between fellow ministry leaders within the same denomination. Good and godly religious leaders became righteously indignant about how someone else chooses to demonstrate their worship for God. Statements are often made like, "Well that's not worship!" and "God never intended people to worship Him like that!"

But it is worship to some people as it is their way of presenting their love and adoration to God. It is not wrong to stand still and sing hymns if you are singing those words to God. Some people say "I just couldn't worship that way." Well, you do not have to. But for those people who choose to express their love to God with hymns they are displaying their love for God. In the same way to dance, clap your hands and wave banners may seem inappropriate to those from a traditional setting when it is the way some of God's children enjoy displaying their love to God. If you find yourself becoming righteously indignant about the way someone else worships, would you stop and tell yourself that maybe this is not such a big issue and maybe you should just . . . let it go.

People who come in to discuss something because of feeling righteous indignation usually have something behind the issue they think they are angry about. In the case of worship there is usually an emotional issue lurking in the background causing them to think of themselves as the worship sheriff sent by God to make sure people worship the way that the law according to them says. It is more about their tradition, than about any spiritual law.

Whatever the issue is from one extreme to the other, even in the middle we can become righteously indignant, down right mad about an issue that God is not indignant about and does not want us to be. You see it in church splits, angry public protests, emails sent to people, phone calls, and complaints about church or government leaders.

The Lord told me that His people get indignant about things; they take offense at things that they should not take offense at. Yet sometimes believers will dive into scripture, dig out their personal view and lay out their argument having all the reasons saying why others should do or believe the way they do, until someone asks about a verse that is not in their argument and messes up everything. Then they have to justify why that verse does not relate to what they are arguing.

Some believers have said that because of a certain sin in another person's life they should not be allowed to minister. Now think about that for a minute. This may have been something that happened years ago. If certain sins keep people from ministry, most local congregations would not allow Paul the apostle to ever minister to them because he had people killed or thrown in jail for believing in Jesus. Yet God forgave him, changed his life and called him to minister for His Kingdom.

Think about King David. Talk about a messed up dysfunctional family, yet God said David was a man after God's own heart. We need to understand this, to get it deep within us. We are not to allow our emotions to cloud what God wants to have happen in people's lives. God wants to allow His mercy and His grace to be poured into people.

My daughter spent a semester while attending American University working with Polaris Project. This Non Governmental Organization (NGO) helps people caught up in human trafficking, especially prostitution be to set free. One of the things the Church needs to learn is that prostitutes are victims of human trafficking. A lot of these people do not want to be involved in prostitution, but their pimps and others will severely punish them if they try to escape to safety.

Many people, even some of our laws over the years, leave us with the impression that if the prostitutes were thrown in jail, the issue would go away. What will have a greater affect will be to arrest the people who go in to commit the acts with the prostitutes. If their names would be posted in the newspaper or there would be some other way of bringing discomfort of this sort into their lives, many of these people would stop pursuing prostitutes. Some nations have found a decrease in prostitution due to arresting and convicting those involved in paying for the acts of prostitution. It seems this is more effective than arresting the pimps and those running brothels.

Spiritual revolution, spiritual climate change comes when the Church rises up to do things differently. Rather than becoming righteously indignant about prostitution we should choose to be like Jesus and see those caught up in prostitution as ones who need mercy and compassion rather than anger. In Matthew 21 Jesus told the Religious Leaders who were prone to act and speak in righteous indignation against Jesus, "Truly I say to you that the tax collectors and *prostitutes* will get into the Kingdom of God before you." So if Jesus was leading the prostitutes into the Kingdom of God, then should we as His followers do the same?

It takes the Church; the Church means all believers in Jesus Christ and not the institutionalized congregations, to rise up and say "This is justice!" If it is important to impact this issue, than the Church will have to realize that being righteously indignant is not the answer to helping these girls and women escape to the freedom of the Kingdom of God like Jesus did. God wants His people to cry out for justice yet we do not seem to do a lot of crying out for justice.

People can speak up for justice without angrily screaming into the wind or into the face of someone else. That just looks a lot like what has become known as righteous indignation. When someone is in a discussion and becomes angry to the point of yelling at you, don't you start to lose some empathy for whatever it is they are discussing with you? Whereas if they are able to express their need without losing control of their emotions, people are more apt to try to help them. Please do not mix up emotional frustration with someone using the excuse of letting their emotions control their outburst of anger and then justifying it by saying they were right or had the right to explode in another person's face over any issue. What's the difference? Being like Jesus. Jesus was able to deal with people and their issues without losing control of his anger and sinning because of it.

In 2 Chronicles 24 there was a King Joash who did what God wanted while a priest named Jehoiada was alive giving him spiritual counsel. Once Jehoiada died, the officials came to King Joash and together they abandoned the temple of the Lord to worship idols. Because of this God's anger came on Judah and Jerusalem. God had sent prophets to warn them, to testify to them that what they were doing was wrong in God's sight. The problem was the people would not listen to what God was saying. Then one day the Spirit of God came on a man named Zechariah who was the son of Jehoiada and he asked the people "Why do you disobey the Lord's commands? You are not going to prosper. You have forsaken the Lord, so He has forsaken you."

Now rather than turn to God they plotted against Zechariah and by order of the King they killed him. The king did not remember all that Zechariah's father had done for him. As king he had felt indignation about what this priest had spoken as the word of God. In his unwillingness to acknowledge what God expected of him and his people, he acted in an angry manner that he felt was right, but it was not.

Remember the account of David, Nabal and Abigail? David felt he was right to be angry with Nabal because he had protected Nabal's sheep and goats. When the sheep shearing time came David wanted Nabal to share his wealth with David and his men for providing protection for Nabal's assets. David became angry and thought that he was right to go down and kill every male that was part of Nabal's family.

Here are two examples of righteous indignation that were only indignation and not righteous at all. You see when people talk about righteous indignation they are saying that someone has become angry and they think they are right to harbor that anger or even to act on it.

In David's case he had taken care of Nabal's sheep and goats but the man never asked him to do that. There was never an agreement between the two. So David was mad because he did something he was not asked to do, yet still felt he had the emotional right to go kick Nabal's family around. Sometimes when our indignation rises up it comes because we have done something we have not been asked to do, out of the goodness of our heart and when we are not acknowledged for it, we get mad about it. So was it really out of the goodness of our heart?

In 1 Samuel 26 King Saul was pursuing David in anger because the people of Israel loved David and King Saul was jealous. David and Abishai, one of his men, were sneaking into Saul's camp. David's men were mad because Saul had been chasing them and threatening to kill them. Abishai wanted to take King Saul's life and it seemed justified. It was not right what the king had been doing and they could end it all right there. The men of David believed all of Israel would rise up and make David king because after all God had already had the prophet Samuel anoint David to be the next king.

Abishai said to David "Today God has given your enemy into your hand, let me take my spear and pin this guy to the ground." He even promised to kill him with one stroke. David responded by pointing out that King Saul too was

God's anointed and when the king's time had come the Lord would take care of him. Even though it seemed like they had the right to kill the king, because they were not being treated justly, David was anointed to take his place. Even though this king was not a godly king, it would have been wrong no matter how indignant they were. To take matters into their own hands would have actually been a demonstration of not trusting God.

At the heart of this discussion about righteous indignation is the question: Are we going to let God deal with issues or are we going to get angry enough about it that we take matters into our own hands and not handle the situation God's way? There will be times God says to do something and you need to act on it. But if you are just angry about something it does not mean God has given you the go ahead to say something or do something to somebody. In David and Abishai's case David was telling Abishai that God would deal with King Saul when God is ready. It was not their place to deal with him.

Some would say that in this account David was only talking about the king because he was anointed. The logic that follows this line of thinking is that it would be okay to do something to someone who is not anointed. If we agree to this mindset we have to go back and ask who does the Bible recognize as anointed. Priests in Exodus 30 and Leviticus 4 were anointed so we would have to cross them off the list of who we could "raise our hand against." Kings were anointed. Prophets (1 Kings 19:16) were anointed. The Messiah in Isaiah 61 was anointed by God's Spirit. Isn't that true of anyone who ministers in a way anointed by Holy Spirit? In Ezekiel 16:9 Cherub's are anointed so angels are anointed too. 2 Corinthians 1:21 where Paul is talking about apostles he says they are anointed. In 1 John 2:20-27 John taught that all believers are anointed. So if the line of thinking is correct then we are not supposed to lift our hands against believers.

There are a lot of people then we are not to do things against who we still let our righteous indignation rise up in opposition to.

What about when you disagree with a politician? Romans 13:1-7 says that God places them in the position they have. You can disagree with them, but do not become "righteously indignant" toward them. You can even become angry with them as long as you deal with your anger even act on it in the way God wants.

What about when you are not being taken care of on a job. Matthew 20:1-6 Jesus shared a parable about a man hiring some people early in the day, others a few hours later, and others toward the end of the day who chose to pay them all the same wage. When the people hired early in the day begin to complain after the employer paid each worker the same wages the employer explained that they were not getting ripped off because he was paying them what he said he would pay them. The point is that God will take care of you. Even when those you work for do not seem to be treating you right. Ask God if He would have you look for a different job, but do not become bitter and angry about it. He may not want you to move on. He may have you there because there is something incredible that you are doing for His Kingdom that you may not be aware of. If that is the case the best place for you to be is right there. The point of the parable is that God will take care of you and everything is God's to give.

When we begin to harbor anger or bitterness because it does not seem fair that someone else has a better job or a newer car than we do, the opportunity arises for the enemy to come in and build up righteous indignation causing our emotional response to turn our hearts from trusting God by claiming that this is just not right. That will lead us to receiving in our souls doubt instead of agreeing with God that He will take care of us. When someone's attitude toward you is wrong, trust God that He can change their heart. Even

179

if God does not change their heart God is growing you into the person He wants you to be; one who can show His mercy and His grace to someone else just as He does to you.

Are you aware of anyone who has a bad attitude toward God? Can you see that God waits and patiently loves them just like He wants us to do if we want to be like Jesus? In Mark 10 the children are being brought to Jesus to have Him touch them. The disciples were trying to turn them away and when Jesus saw this He was indignant with them. It is not always wrong to be indignant. What the disciples were doing by trying to keep the children away from Him was wrong. He told them that the Kingdom of Heaven belonged to such as these children. He took the children in His arms and blessed them.

There are times when being indignant is the right way to feel; to sense when you can do something about a wrong to make it right. When that time occurs, and you can respond like Jesus would, you should act righteously. If it is not within your power to change that situation then you should trust God rather than let yourself become angrier and angrier.

People who believe they have a right to act with righteous indignation almost always believe they are right and they are helping God when in reality God does not need our help in that situation. Yet there are times when it is right to be indignant and there are a few ways we can respond in the right way. Please know that when indignation is right it has come from God. It is what we do with it that may make it wrong.

We need to start thinking differently when our emotions rise up and we become indignant. Instead of allowing anger to overcome us we need to learn to laugh more. To realize that rather than become so angry that our emotions take over, we need to let many issues go, to learn to enjoy life more and not be uptight as Christians. Let's enjoy the God we serve and the life He has given us and learn to laugh more.

I know there are things that happen that just are not right, but we can still trust God when things are not right. If we seek God more and ask Him how He would have us act so we do not sin, we will enjoy life more knowing that something good can come out of whatever it is we have become so upset about. Rather than get angry, choose to pray that God will touch people by changing and reconciling the situation.

Emotionally we want what we think is best for us and those we know. It might not be what God knows is best for us or the people we know. God may seem to act like a parent who allows his children to make decisions that might not be the best for their child because their child will learn to decide differently next time. We may have wondered why someone did not stop us from doing something in the past but God had something for us to learn. When something goes wrong at school God may want you to work with a teacher or administrator to help win their heart rather than go to deal with the situation from an attitude of "righteous indignation". We as believers need to demonstrate the love and mercy of God to everyone because that is what Jesus would do.

So we need to treat people like Jesus treated people. Proverbs 10:12 tells us that hatred stirs up dissension but love covers over all wrongs. We need to cover over people's wrongs more. It means we go to them privately to help bring correction. I know of a man who went privately to another man who had publicly rebuked someone. The first man took him aside privately to restore him by correcting the way he had chosen to publicly address another man's issue. He also learned that next time he would just walk over and gently pull the person acting in this way aside to gently say, "That's not the best way to handle this."

We need to trust God to provide and take care of us. The Righteous Indignation Syndrome costs people more than we possibly know. It costs one's reputation, often relationships, a person's testimony and even the opportunity to be more like Jesus. Besides others may know that anger is not a fruit of the Spirit so they know that the one acting in the Righteous Indignation Syndrome is not walking in the Spirit but in the flesh.

In Exodus 32:9-10 after the people of Israel had made the golden calf, the Lord told Moses to leave Him alone so His anger could burn against them and He would destroy them. We need to realize that we are made in the image of God and there are times that even God can become so angry about something that if He is left alone His anger will burn to the point that His justice will be displayed in a certain way. Yet Moses did not leave God alone. He told Him that while God had the right to justly punish them; it would impact what the nations would say about God. Moses did not leave God alone. When we are left alone with our anger, our anger burns in us, just like it does in God. Since it was true of God and He always acts justly, we must not allow our emotions to control us causing us to act wrongly. If I want to be like Jesus, then I will know when to pull back and act like Jesus would.

Finally, at the heart of anger is a lack of forgiveness. Angry people have a heart issue that makes them angry. They become angry because of something they have in their heart and they choose to take it out on someone else. That does not justify what they do, but it tells us that if someone is an angry person they need God to heal them of the anger in their life. That person needs to stop trying to justify the anger by declaring it as righteous indignation. The anger might be there because of something that happened as a child or as an adult. It may have started when things did not go the way they wanted, or by God not coming through for them like they thought He should.

If we deal with anger correctly God will be advanced in everyone's life. Righteous indignation in most people's lives is just emotion out of control. If you have found lately that you are getting more and more angry about things, God wants to set you free from the anger. Do not confuse when Holy Spirit is stirring within you because something is wrong with your being angry and giving in to your own emotions. If you have an anger issue, it comes up, it boils over. You may be calm one minute and ready to erupt in anger the next. God wants to deal not only with how easily people become angry but how quickly they act on the anger.

Even if this has been true of you, God is not standing in heaven pointing His finger down at you saying "If you don't change I am so going to zap you." He's not an angry God, He is good. He sees people's angry heart and is saying to them "If you have an angry heart I want to bless you with a gentle and loving heart. If things that have happened to you in the past had planted the seed of anger in your heart, I want to remove the very root of it. Because you keep cutting it off like a weed, but you have not gotten the root out." He wants to reach deep within your heart and pull out the root and replace it with peace. Why not set this book down and ask God to deal with the root of anger in your life right now.

If you know of people who have the need for God to remove the root of anger from their heart, take some time to pray for God to move in their heart and replace the anger with peace. For the peace of God changes us from the inside out.

## Chapter 10

# The "Unworthy" Syndrome

The story is told of two 90 year old men, Moe and Joe, who have been friends all of their lives. When it's clear that Joe is dying, Moe visits him every day. One day Moe says, "Joe, we both loved baseball all our lives, and we played minor league ball together for so many years. Please do me one favor, when you get to Heaven, somehow you must let me know if there's baseball there."

Joe looks up at Moe from his death bed, "Moe, you've been my best friend for many years. If it's at all possible, I'll do this favor for you."

Shortly after that, Joe passes on. At midnight a couple of nights later, Moe is awakened from a sound sleep by a blinding flash of white light and a voice calling out to him, "Moe—Moe."

"Who is it?" asks Moe sitting up suddenly. "Who is it?"

"Moe—it's me, Joe."

"You're not Joe. Joe just died."

"I'm telling you, it's me, Joe," insists the voice.

"Joe! Where are you?"

"In heaven," replies Joe. "I have some really good news and a little bad news."

"Tell me the good news first," says Moe.

"The good news," Joe says, "is that there's baseball in heaven. Better yet, all of our old buddies who died before us are here, too. Better than that, we're all young again. Better still, it's always spring time and it never rains or snows. And best of all, we can play baseball all we want, and we never get tired."

"That's fantastic," says Moe. "It's beyond my wildest dreams! So what's the bad news?"

"You're pitching Tuesday."

Here's the thing – if this were true, even if Moe didn't feel worthy of pitching in heaven, he would still be pitching.

This is a problem in the Church today. No matter how much we hear it, we still listen and agree with the lie that says we are not worthy. We believe we are not worthy of all the things God wants to do in our lives, of all the blessings He wants to pour out into our lives.

Someone once said, "Feelings are just feelings and sometimes they reflect the truth but often they don't." Yet too many believers in Jesus Christ live as if they are unworthy because they feel as if they are insignificant and without value in the Kingdom of God. Because we have felt that way for so long . . . we just believe it and have come into agreement with it.

Ask yourself, "Have I ever felt unworthy of God and what He wants to do in my life?" Maybe even what God has called you to do? Perhaps a better question is "Do I feel that way today?" Recently at a gathering one of the leaders present shared how he felt so unworthy. So we asked the group gathered "How many of you feel unworthy," and over half the people stood up. These were people of God. People who have given their lives to Jesus, many who have a close relationship with God, stood and said "I just do not feel worthy."

This happens because we have come into agreement with the spirit of religion that has pounded on us for so long. It has produced a mindset that God is always looking for some reason to be mad at us and He only wants to punish us or thump on us. The reality is the Bible says God wants to bless us.

If you are a believer you need to know that you are worthy and of value to the Lord. Would you stop reading and say out loud: "I am worthy and of value to the Lord."

There are these feelings, these emotions of unworthiness that are often taught to us as we are young and growing up. We have received them from people's statements about our lives, and into our lives. There are actions that have been taken against us by people that have caused us to feel unworthy. There are times that people speak incredibly positive statements into our lives. The opposite of that is when people speak negative statements into our lives that cause us to feel we are not worthy.

Unworthiness is based on not knowing or believing God enough to trust Him in everything. We hold onto feelings of unworthiness because we do not know God enough or trust God enough that when He says we are worthy we believe Him. We are worthy to be part of His Kingdom and all the blessings He wants to pour out in our lives. Unworthiness is based in our lack of belief and feelings.

Feelings come and go. Sometimes if we sit down and wait long enough a feeling will pass. People have so bought into allowing their emotions to control and govern their lives that they believe they are unworthy of God and a lot of other things that God never intended us to think.

In the book of Judges there are a couple of examples of people who did not think they were worthy, but God said they were. In chapter 4 the people of Israel were once again doing what they had been doing before and it was evil in God's eyes. There was a king of Canaan who had cruelly oppressing the Israelites for twenty years. So they cried to the Lord for help. Why did it take them twenty years to cry for help? Why does it take us so song to say "Oh God I need you to help me?" It is often because we do not think we are worthy of God helping us.

In this circumstance the Lord had the prophetess Deborah leading Israel at the time. Did you catch that? She was a prophetess, called of God to speak the heart of God and she was leading Israel, the chosen people of God. While she was holding court, the Israelites came to her to have their disputes decided – she was acting as their judge. In the midst of this picture Deborah sent for a man named Barak. The Bible does not tell us if he was a commander of the army or a carpenter, it only tells us that she sent for him and gave him a command to take ten thousand men with him from two of the tribes of Israel. When the Lord drew out Sisera who was the commander of the King of Canaan's army, the Lord was going to give him and the army into Barak's hands.

So there it was. The woman of God, the prophetess who was ruling over all of Israel, called this man out. Barak responded in an unworthy manner. He said he would go if she would go with him, but if she would not go with him, he was not going. Wait a minute, had God not called him out to do this? Then why wouldn't he do what God wanted? Because there was a fear there that God would not do what He said He would do. Barak thought of himself as unworthy. Barak did not trust God enough to take him at His word, yet God had chosen Barak. Therefore Barak was worthy to accomplish this task for God. Did you get that? Even though he thought he was unworthy, he was worthy.

God had called Barak out of whatever was going on in his life and told him, "This is what I have called you to do." We do not know anything about Barak, at least the scripture does not tell us if he was an incredibly godly man or not, yet here he was saying to the prophetess, "I'll only do this if you will go with me." In a day when women were not looked on favorably as leaders, when men wanted to be acknowledged for what they did, this man would only move out and do what God had commanded him to do, if she would go with him. The picture speaks to a man who felt unworthy.

Deborah agreed to go with him but told him that because of how he was going about this, the honor would not be his because God was going to allow another woman to deal with Sisera who was the commander of the army. So off they went together and when Barak summoned the men of these two tribes, ten thousand men rose up and came with him, along with Deborah.

As the Lord had me traveling around the state of Washington calling on each of the twelve regions within our state calling for gatherings of the apostolic and prophetic people in each region, not many people would stand up and say "I'll set a date, I'll call the people to come." There were few who felt worthy to step up and say "I'll do it for the Lord." So the Lord had me say to individuals "you are the one to call for this gathering." They often would respond with "I don't know what to do." With great faith in what God had told us to do I would tell them: "You set a date and a time. Start contacting apostolic and prophetic people to come, they will invite others to come and they will come." We spoke this to a lady in the fifth region of our state, she agreed and fifty four people showed up. A man in the tenth region stepped up and ninety eight people showed up for their first gathering. In region nine with the smallest population of the 12 regions when one man agreed to call these people to come, 40 plus showed up. Why did people come? Because someone said, "Yes Lord, I'll do it."

After six months of talking with one man who knew he was supposed to call for the gathering in his region, he set the date and called the people in his region and 40 showed up. Four months into talking with him he told me "You must think I'm the slowest one, like a slug or something." He just had some issues he needed to work through. One of those was whether he was worthy to take on this assignment from God.

In the same way God has called you to do something for His Kingdom and perhaps there is a sense of unworthiness that is keeping you from doing something He has called you to do. You know that Jesus lives in you right? The Bible says "I have been crucified with Christ. It is no longer I who live but Christ lives in me and the life I now live in the flesh I live by faith in the Son of God who loved me and gave Himself up for me." (Galatians 2:20) You should memorize that verse, because it is about you and the fact that Jesus lives in you, so you are worthy in the eyes of God. Whether you are an 8 year old or you are in your 80's God has assignments for you to do and it is often the feeling of unworthiness that holds you back from stepping into that. The excuses people use are abundant – "I couldn't do that. There are people who are more qualified."

In Judges 6 a young man named Gideon was called out of his daily life by an angel who said to him "The Lord is with you O valiant warrior." Gideon was hiding in a wine press beating out wheat to hide it from the Midianites who were ravaging the land. Valiant warrior? Come on, this guy was hiding; God could not have meant that Gideon was a valiant warrior. Even Gideon did not believe it. He kept testing God to see if what the angel had said would come true because he was asking God "Who am I?" That is a sure sign of unworthiness when someone says to God, the Creator of the universe, the maker and Lord of everyone "Who am I God, you must have made a mistake." Again and again God demonstrated to Gideon that he indeed was the one God had called to lead the people of Israel and deliver them from the hands of their enemies.

When the angel appeared to him, Gideon started questioning the angel. Now think about if an angel came to bring you a message from God. Should that tell you that God thinks of you as worthy to accomplish what He is planning to do through you? Gideon asked, "If the LORD is with us, why then has all this happened to us?" It had happened because the people had quit doing what God wanted them to do. Then he said, "And where are all His miracles which our fathers told us about, saying, 'Did not the LORD bring us up from Egypt?' But now the LORD has abandoned us and given us into the hand of Midian." The Lord does not abandon people; they just come to a place in their lives where they feel unqualified, unable to do what God wants ever again. They feel unworthy. BUT that is not true.

In Judges 6 and 7 Gideon needed reassurances to act on God's behalf. He asked for a fleece that he placed on the grass to be dry in the morning with only the ground wet from the dew. God did it. That was not enough for Gideon so he asked for the fleece to be wet and for the ground to be dry the next morning and God did that as well. God knew Gideon's heart was not ready to act. It took Gideon and another man sneaking into spy out the enemy's camp and hearing of a dream one of the Midianites had with the explanation being that Gideon was going to come and defeat them before Gideon believed that he was worthy to act on God's behalf. He needed reassurances. Have you ever needed God to reassure you in order for you to act on God's behalf? You are still worthy, but sometimes you may forget that.

Feelings of unworthiness work in agreement with guilt and shame. These feelings often come as a result of not forgiving yourself, not believing God has forgiven you or not believing God has more for you. It is all about believing God. If you haven't forgiven yourself you are still taking the blame for things you did that God has already forgiven you of. Remember if you confess your sins God is faithful and just to forgive you of your sins? So God has already forgiven you of your confessed sins – yet the enemy works to get you to agree with guilt and shame to keep you from advancing God's Kingdom through your life.

There was a lady who told me how she had confessed something to the Lord and the thoughts that she was unworthy kept coming back to her. She would rebuke the thoughts by telling them she did not agree with them, that God had forgiven her. For a week she battled with the thoughts that kept coming back to her until she won the battle and finally it lifted and it is not a struggle now. When the enemy comes against you, and know that he will come, and come and come until he is defeated. If you have taken a stand against thoughts of unworthiness before and yet have given into them, the enemy will keep coming after you until you stand and do not give the same ground back by rebuking the thoughts until they stop coming. This is true of what you think and believe about yourself.

God says you are worthy so when the enemy comes against you telling you that you are unworthy you have to say "That's not true, I will not agree with those words." If you have been agreeing with them, know that there is going to be a battle to stop agreeing with them. Determine that you will intentionally stop agreeing with what the enemy has been saying to you. If you do not take this kind of a stand you will end up settling for so much less than God intends for you to have because you believe that you do not deserve it. If you do not believe you deserve it, then you have bought into the lie that you are unworthy. But know this, you do deserve good things from God and you are worthy of His love, His goodness and His glory to be seen through your life. You deserve it because Jesus died on the cross for you. By Jesus dying you are able to receive what He has done and by receiving Him as your Lord and Savior you have become a child of God, a prince or princess in the Kingdom of the Most High God. We forget that. We need to be reminded of it until the truth that we are already in Jesus Christ becomes so prominent in our souls that this truth takes over our lives as well as what we believe about ourselves.

There are people who do not believe they are worthy to be healed. You see it when they are asked if they are willing to be prayed for and they either turn down prayer or do not believe healing will happen to them. So when God heals them they are shocked because they do not think or believe they are worthy to be healed. Those emotions are so real. They rise up to overcome what you know to be true and hinder you from living in the fullness of God's blessings in your life. Do you ask God to bless you? Does it seem easier to ask God to bless others? Many people find it difficult to ask God to bless them. Do you? Ask yourself why?

Isn't it amazing how long of a list children will bring to their parents for Christmas presents? They have no problem asking their parents to bless them. When you come to God, do you ask Him to bless you? If not, it is because you have come into agreement with the thought that you are unworthy to be blessed by God. Feelings of unworthiness to be blessed, whether the blessing be physical, financial, relational, or by healing – come because you do not believe God loves you for who you are. These feelings cause you to think you must have to do something to earn God's love before He will bless you. But if that were the case, then you would have to do something to earn your salvation before God would extend it to you. Yet all you had to do was say "Jesus I want you to be my Lord and Savior" and He freely gave you salvation.

Feelings of unworthiness cause you to do things you have always done that are no longer consistent with whom God says you are. When you know you are worthy you will take on responsibilities for God's Kingdom due to your signifi-cance because you are acting as a good steward. It is not who you are, but who Jesus is in you that makes you significant to do what He wants. When you know you are worthy in the Kingdom of God you believe what you do is important, it is for the King and for your future. So you minister knowing that what you do in the Kingdom is significant and that it helps others grow spiritually. It is not just about surviving personally now; you are about advancing the Kingdom of God.

When you know you are worthy of the Kingdom of God you praise God because you trust Him to take care of you, to provide for you, for you know God will not fail you. "Feelings are just feelings." Sometimes they reflect the truth; often they don't. Someone once said "If my friends misled me as much as my emotions, they would not be my friend." So why do we live by our emotions?

Your emotions themselves are from God; they are a part of the image of God in you, yet God never meant for your feelings to be the standard of your life or to determine how you live it. Your feelings do not define you; they are not designed to interpret or understand the situations you now face. Only God's Spirit and truth can define your worthiness, and guide you through the circumstances of your life. **You are not your emotions** – You are defined by God, not your emotions. You may not feel like it, but God says you are worthy of His love and His blessings in your life. He loves you no matter what you've done.

The Lord told me that "My people do not believe they are worthy because they do not feel they are worthy, therefore they believe lies." The problem is that we come into agreement with our spiritual enemy who continues to tell us we are not worthy. But God tells us we are worthy. In John 10:10 Jesus said that the enemy comes to steal, to destroy and to kill. He wants to destroy our understanding of who we are in Jesus Christ, of whom God says we are and cause us to not feel worthy to do anything for the Kingdom of God. Have you ever experienced that feeling? As I talk with people this is clearly a tactic of the enemy to keep God's people from advancing God's Kingdom.

While our emotions are definitely part of the image of God in us, as we learn to control them and learn to move as God wants us to then we do not have to give into those feelings of unworthiness.

God also said "My people do not feel worthy because of what someone else did to them and they just cannot forgive themselves." If you have dealt with anyone who has been abused in any way it will become clear they usually take on the responsibility for what has been done to them. They think and often verbalize, "If I had done this differently this person would not have said these things. This person would not have done these things to me so it must be my fault." That is what abuse does to people, it just keeps hammering into people's spirit and soul that they are the one that is guilty, that they are the one responsible for everything that has taken place in their life.

We need to put responsibility where it belongs. It belongs on the person who has done the abusing. Most of the time in spousal abuse and victims of prostitution it takes seven or eight times for a victim to actually step out of the abusive relationship and receive help. Talking with a woman who was being slapped around by her boyfriend I told her she should not stay in that relationship and put up with the abuse. She went through a litany of reasons it was her fault. "I should not be doing this. . . I push his buttons and if I did not push his buttons he would not act that way." I used a theological expression with her to help her to see that her reasoning was inaccurate. I said to her "That's baloney, that is just baloney. Nobody . . . nobody has their buttons pushed so far that they have to respond in that kind of anger. If they do there is a spirit of anger in their life and they need to get help, as well as the person being abused."

Even knowing this, people still have not been able to get over that feeling of unworthiness. But God says it starts with forgiving the other person. Many people ask how is someone able to forgive another for what they have done. Because they want to be like Jesus and Jesus was able to say while hanging on the cross "Father forgive them for they do not know what they are doing." These were the people who abused Him physically and then hung Him on the cross.

Forgiving someone does not require the same level of trust for the person. Trust is different than forgiveness. You can forgive someone for what they did to you so you can move on in life and then your healing can start. You need to come to the place where you realize who you are in Jesus and the fact that what the person has done to you doesn't change who you are in Christ Jesus. When you come to the place where you can forgive the person and begin walking in the truth of who you are in Jesus, those feelings will begin to lift.

You will have to battle through that. It usually will not be a one time declaration of "those battles have to leave me, Amen." The enemy will keep coming back because this area of your life is a stronghold he does not want to give up. A stronghold is something you have come into agreement with the enemy to believe that has a strong hold on you. When you no longer agree with the enemy, when you choose to believe differently, when you come into agreement with God, and when you choose to believe what God has said – the enemy will fight not to lose the ground he worked to gain and maintain in your life. For you to walk in your worthiness you have to keep repelling those thoughts that come against you by recognizing these attacks and telling the thoughts in Jesus' name to leave.

While talking with someone recently about their struggle with verbal spousal abuse they told me that it took them about a week of continual warfare, of continual not giving in, not coming into agreement with those thoughts that had been saying that the person was unworthy and that the person deserved what happened to them for that suddenly to break off of them. If you prayed once and it did not go away, do not stop. Keep exerting your authority in Jesus. You will win the battle and it will eventually break off of you. You may need to find people who will come alongside you who will pray with you and for you during this time. Ask them to constantly pray for you: every time you come to their mind to pray for you. When an attack comes against you in your mind, you say to the Lord: "Wake up those intercessors! Put my name in their thoughts." The Lord will answer this prayer.

There are people who have agreed to pray for us whenever God brings my family or me to their mind. So there are times in the middle of the night or during the day when I will cry out to God to wake up the intercessors. I have explained to those who have agreed to pray for us that when we come to their mind, when they wake up during the night and we are on their mind that it is Holy Spirit moving in their spirit or stirring them up. They recognize this as their need to start praying and not to stop until Holy Spirit releases them. They have realized that if they are sensing anger toward me when I have done nothing to cause this feeling then anger is probably coming against me. Then they can target their prayers to put an end to anger's attack. Particularly if they remember they have not seen me all day and are asking themselves "why would I be mad at him?"

When your spouse or a friend comes to your mind and you have not seen them for hours or possibly days it is Holy Spirit stirring you up to pray for that person. Holy Spirit is telling you that an attack is coming against them and you need to focus your spirit on praying for them and against the attack sent to get them off track with what God wants them to be doing. The sense of being lonely or isolated may not be coming against you, but it may be coming against the person that God has brought to your mind.

These types of attacks will come against your feeling worthy or believing you are worthy. The enemy of your soul will use your emotions to manipulate you into thinking and then believing that God does not love you and God does not care.

In Colossians 3:12-14 the Bible says "So, as those who have been chosen of God, holy and beloved, put on a heart of compassion, kindness, humility, gentleness and patience; bearing with one another, and forgiving each other, whoever has a complaint against anyone; just as the Lord forgave you, so also should you. Beyond all these things put on love, which is the perfect bond of unity."

When God brings someone to your mind it is because He loves that person. If you are concerned that you are going to be praying all day long, remember that you do not have to pray for an hour about each person who comes to your mind. If you are sensing isolation and loneliness, pray something like this: "Lord, people come to my mind, and so has a sense of feeling lonely and isolated and I ask you to break this off of them and replace it with peace. I ask that you would stand and protect them and give the assurance that they are loved by you and by others. That you would have others who would call and encourage them and they would feel encouraged by the power of Jesus' name."

Then you are done and are able to move on, unless Holy Spirit presses you. You will know when Holy Spirit presses you because He does not let you go. You will have the sense that you cannot stop praying. You do not have to pray out loud. God hears the prayers of our spirit.

The Lord also said "My people do not believe they are worthy so they do not feel they are worthy because sometimes they do not make the right choices." When we do not make the right choice the enemy comes against us and begins manipulating our emotions by saying to us, "You sinned, you did not do what God wanted so you are not worthy of God's love." That is a lie to stir you up emotionally in order to move you into agreement with the lie. The strategy of the enemy is to get you to begin to question whether God could ever forgive you as well as bring doubt that God will ever use you again.

That is just a lie. We are children of the King. We are loved by the King. Any child who comes to the King of Glory and says "Father I did this and it was wrong," the Bible says immediately that child of God is forgiven. The enemy does not want the King's children to believe they are forgiven.

The enemy's tactic is a lot like the scene from the movie Rocky 3 where "Clubber Lang" keeps throwing Rocky into the corner of the boxing ring to beat on him some more. Many times believers in Jesus feel like they keep getting thrown into the corner of a boxing ring and the enemy just keeps beating on them. The reason this tactic works in many lives is because even though God has forgiven us, we do not fully believe we are forgiven, we do not believe we are worthy of God's love. So we continue to allow the enemy to push us into a corner and heap shame, condemnation and guilt on us for something the King of Glory, our heavenly Father, has already forgiven.

The enemy enjoys manipulating us by using our emotions and feelings to tell us we are not worthy of God's love. We need to draw near to God and He will draw near to us. He will keep us away from the thoughts of the enemy and entrenched in the love of Father God.

Yet sometimes our choices impact what we know to be true in our spirit based on the word of God. In Matthew 10:37-39 we find a couple of interesting verses that fly in the face of where our nation and God's Church finds themselves today. In these verses Jesus says: "He who loves father or mother more than Me is not worthy of Me; and he who loves son or daughter more than Me is not worthy of Me. And he who does not take his cross and follow after Me is not worthy of Me. He who has found his life will lose it, and he who has lost his life for My sake will find it." Sometimes we do not feel worthy because instead of having God be our highest priority, our highest love we allow a family member to become more important, or we allow our family to become more important than Jesus.

Jesus may tell you He wants you to do something but if it conflicts with the family schedule and you choose the family schedule over what Jesus has told you to do – according to this verse, at that point, you probably will begin not to feel worthy of what God wants. Yet it takes a simple correction, telling the Lord "I'll do whatever you want me to do," and then doing it. Remember in Matthew 21 there is a parable of a father speaking to two sons and telling them to go work in the vineyard? The first son said "No, I'm not going to do that" and then changed his mind and went anyway and worked in the vineyard. The second son said, "I'll go" and then did not go. Which of those two people did what his father wanted? The first one did because even though he said he would not go, he went and did what the father wanted. There may have been times in your life when God said "Go do this" and you may have said "No, I won't do it." But then later you remembered and you did obey. By later it may be weeks or months later. No matter how long you may have waited, if you will go do what God has told you to do, the feelings of unworthiness will begin to lift. Because you have shifted into the mindset that you will do what God has told you to do.

If you have a friendship in which your friend has begun to feel unworthy of your friendship due to decisions they have made, even if you tell them you want the friendship to continue – they have to make the choice to believe you and to pursue that relationship. But because people feel unworthy they do not step into relationships God wants them to have. The enemy is feeding the thoughts that "If they find out who you are, it will be worse than if you had never started the relationship with them." The people who are true friends know who we are and love us anyway.

The same is true of our relationship with God. God continues to want you to believe Him that you are worthy of His love and He just loves us. When we choose not to pursue God, feelings of unworthiness pursue us and cause us to think we are not worthy of God's love. We allow these to keep us from being who God wants us to be. We stop believing we are worthy of being His children and our relationship with Father God spirals down the drain of life.

People do not understand how important they are to God. Do you personally? Do you know how important you are to God? Jesus died for you. Don't let that fall away from you; embrace the fact that God loves you so much Jesus died for you. You are worthy because God created you according to Psa. 139. You are worthy because whether you feel like it or not He says you are worthy. You are worthy because you were created in His image.

# Chapter 11

# The "Manipulating Other's Emotions with My Emotions" Syndrome

When we believe and live like we are unworthy it is easy to have our emotions manipulated by other people. When we believe we are unworthy it is easier to be manipulated by our spiritual enemies as well. There are demonic powers that come against you and speak to you in order to convince you not to do what God has told you to do.

There may be a special meeting where people are getting together to worship God and to learn together and God tells you to attend and you believe you ought to go. Yet that afternoon rolls around, and many circumstances do not work the way they are supposed to and you are at home. The meeting is in about an hour and that voice in your head says "You should just stay home and rest. If you go tonight it's just not going to be worth it. Besides, you are not worthy to be there with those people." You struggle with going. The voice may say other things, but the enemy is doing to you exactly what you are allowing them to do and that is, manipulate your emotions.

The good news is you can choose not to be manipulated by other people's emotions and you can choose not to be spiritually manipulated. If you are a person who manipulates others, you can choose to stop and let the Spirit of God move in people's lives instead.

Has anyone ever said: "You can't guilt me into doing that"? Have you ever thought that? That is not allowing someone to manipulate your emotions.

"You don't have to come, it is okay. It's not like we have not done anything for you before. You don't have to make that special salad for the family gathering; it is okay – just one more thing I have to do as your mother. But because I love you I'll do that."

Think of ways people manipulate others at work. "Would you do this for me? I just . . . I just have so much to do." You look at your desk and there's a high stack of assignments you have to do and on their desk there's a short stack. "I just don't . . . I'm not feeling well." All of a sudden it is not just a question of could you help me out, but now they have begun manipulating your emotions. There is a difference between asking someone for help, which is alright to do, and asking the question when bringing with it emotional turmoil. Perhaps the request is followed by "I have done an awful lot for you lately. Just this morning I got you a cup of coffee on the way in to work, incidentally you still owe me three dollars for that." Perhaps you recognize the emotional tones that are attached to these requests that manipulate people.

Emotional manipulation is a result of being in bondage to other people's emotions. When you are so angry with a person that you cannot forgive them, they have you in bondage by your own emotions. When just thinking about someone sets you off, then you are in emotional bondage to that person.

It has been said that in the case of men, if one walks into their home you will usually not find pictures of his parents.

If you do not, that man is in emotional bondage to his parents. The same reality must be true of the wife – if there are no pictures of her parents in the house then she too is in emotional bondage to her parents because they do not want to put the pictures up. The person does not want the reminder of their parents constantly before them in their home. Then when the parents come over the one in emotional bondage will usually hear statements like "Didn't we give you a picture for Christmas? Because I'm not seeing it anywhere, I was sure we did." Those two sentences alone demonstrate emotional manipulation and are effective because the person is in emotional bondage to their parent which allows them to be easily manipulated.

Some of the most effective manipulators I have ever met are under the age of seven. It seems like they do not even know what they are doing. They can get away with it because they are so cute. Not to pick on children, but watch what happens when a child comes in wanting something from the adults in the room, or at a store.

Every television commercial you see intends to manipulate your emotions. You may be old enough to remember the slogan, "You deserve a break today, so get up and get away to . . . McDonalds." Let's take that statement apart. "You deserve a break today. . . ." We were being told that our day has been so tough that we deserve to treat ourselves to something special. "So get up and get away . . . ." The slogan is playing on how you feel and is telling you that you can treat yourself to something "good" without having to spend hundreds of dollars. You do not have to buy into these tactics.

Why do you think they show the food commercials late at night? If you have decided not to eat snacks late at night inevitably a commercial comes on TV advertising some food or local restaurant where everyone is having a fun time. One of the first thoughts that will come into your mind will be

205

"You know, tonight it would not be a bad idea. After all, that fast food restaurant is open until midnight. Some restaurants have a drive through window that is open all night. I could minister to my wife by buying her a, uh . . . Chalupa. And if I bought a meal deal it would save money . . . ." It just takes off on us all because a commercial has enticed our flesh by planting an emotional seed of manipulation with us which says, "We have what you want, what you need and it's available right now!"

People use their emotions to get their family members to do what they want. They may cry, blame each other when they have failed, or they make life miserable until they get their own way. People use their emotions by using guilt. They may use fear to control the emotions of another individual or group of individuals to get what they want, even just to get others to agree with them.

If you have ever seen the musical "The Music Man" there is a vivid example of people's emotions being manipulated by fear. The lead character Harold Hill is a con man that comes to a little town of River City, Iowa. His plan is to find a way to con or manipulate the town's people into buying instruments and band uniforms for their town. Yet in order to convince these people to do something they neither want nor need to do, Harold Hill has to discover a way to manipulate their emotions to get them to think this is an important thing to do. So he sings a song about a pool hall. All through this song is the phrase "We've got trouble, right here in River City. That starts with 'T' and rhymes with 'P' and stands for pool." He shares a litany of troubling actions of those who hang out at the Pool Hall. They smoke, they cuss . . . "Kids are going to come home hearing these words, speaking these words. . . ."

During this song the whole town gets themselves worked up by the description of what might happen at the Pool Hall which has one billiard table. Harold explains how this is going to lead the entire town's youth astray from good morals. They work themselves into an emotional frenzy that allows him to say "What we need here is a band!" The town all yells in agreement that this must be the answer. Having freaked out by allowing their emotions to become manipulated, they follow this man down this road thinking this will save their young people. Even though this is a movie, people react in a similar way all the time when they think they have to protect their young people from doing something.

All of this again demonstrates that our emotions can come into bondage to another person's emotions whether that may be parents, family members, fellow employees, bosses or church people. We can be emotionally in bondage to someone because we do not take the time to stop and ask "God, what do you want me to do?"

People also use their emotions to manipulate others to back down. "If you don't do this, we'll leave. If you do this, I'll never be your friend again. If you share Jesus with people you'll be fired." These are just a couple of examples of people using "if" followed by a threat to manipulate another person. Often "if" is used to get people to back down from their convictions and their commitments. Acts 21:8-14 gives us an example of this. Paul was on his way to Jerusalem. He and the group of people with him were voyaging to different places on their way to see friends. At verse 8 Luke wrote and gave this account.

"On the next day we left and came to Caesarea, and entering the house of Philip the evangelist, who was one of the seven, we stayed with him. Now this man had four virgin daughters who were prophetesses. As we were staying there for some days, a prophet named Agabus came down from Judea. And coming to us, he took Paul's belt and bound his own feet and hands, *(Picture that, what a vivid illustration to get the people's attention)* and said, "This is what the Holy Spirit says: 'In this way the Jews at Jerusalem will bind the man who owns this belt and deliver him into the hands of the Gentiles.' When we had heard this, we as well as the local residents began *begging* him not to go up to Jerusalem. Then Paul answered, 'What are you doing, *weeping and breaking my heart*? For I am ready not only to be bound, but even to die at Jerusalem for the name of the Lord Jesus.' And since he would not be persuaded, we fell silent, remarking, 'The will of the Lord be done!'" (I added the emphasis with bold and italics.)

They were using their heart desire to manipulate Paul by begging him. Imagine them almost crying as they pleaded with Paul. "We don't want to see you bound, we don't want to see this happen to you."

Yet Paul challenged their manipulation by acknowledging that they were weeping and breaking his heart. Then he reminded them of his calling and responsibility to do whatever it was God has told him to do.

The Bible says "since he would not be persuaded, we fell silent." They kept after him until they finally gave up. These were people who loved Jesus. But because they did not want Paul to suffer even though he knew God had told him to go do this, they kept after him. You can almost hear them saying, "Don't go, don't go. . . don't go!" Knowing him to be a man who would do what God wanted, they were still trying to persuade him – yet he would not give in because going to Jerusalem was what the Lord wanted. What they did was manipulating someone's emotions, pleading with him.

These were good church people who were the Apostle Paul's friends. "Don't go!!" they cried. Yet Paul was talking with God – "Wait a minute God, you told me to go to Jerusalem." During this short conversation with God Paul was hearing from his friends – "But they are going to tie you up there. There is so much more God must have for you to do." Paul must have found it necessary to remind them,

"It doesn't matter, this is what God told me to do and I'm willing to die for the name of Jesus."

Do you see how our emotions play such a controlling factor in what we do? In 1 Samuel 20 verses 24-34 there is another account of this syndrome. David knew that King Saul was trying to kill him so he was unwilling to go to a feast that the king required of his people. Jonathan who was both David's best friend and the King's son was having a difficult time believing that his father wanted to kill his friend. It's interesting that even today people closest to manipulators do not usually see the manipulation is happening because they have been manipulated all their lives. So in verse 27 the account relates what happened.

"Why has the son of Jesse not come to the meal, either yesterday or today?" Jonathan then answered Saul, "David earnestly asked leave of me to go to Bethlehem, for he said, 'Please let me go, since our family has a sacrifice in the city, and my brother has commanded me to attend. And now, if I have found favor in your sight, please let me get away that I may see my brothers.' For this reason he has not come to the king's table."

Now it seems that this was a reasonable request on the part of David. But Saul's anger then rose up against Jonathan and he responded to his own son. "You son of a perverse, rebellious woman! Do I not know that you are choosing the son of Jesse to your own shame and to the shame of your mother's nakedness?"

This is one of the strategies of people who manipulate. They will try to use guilt and shame to control the emotional response and reaction of others. He then used another part of the strategy of manipulators in verse 31, "For as long as the son of Jesse lives on the earth, neither you nor your kingdom will be established. Therefore now, send and bring him to me, for he must surely die."

The king said if you don't do what I say it is going to cause you problems. He told Jonathan if they did not get rid of David, he would never be the king! David was going to affect everything! Jonathan got up from the table to argue his opinion and his own father then threw a spear at him. Doesn't that seem to be more of a detriment to becoming the next king, a spear thrown by your own father that pierces your body and kills you than being loyal to a friend?

All through scripture there are story lines that if you stop and ask what happened here, you will see example after example of people trying to emotionally manipulate someone else. The strategy is to convince someone that if he does not agree with them then something bad is going to take place in his life. He has to agree with them even though it runs contrary to what he knows he is supposed to do. In the case of Jonathan he knew what he was supposed to do. He had made a covenant with David in which they had agreed to take care of each other and each other's families should something happen to one of them. Jonathan knew what God wanted him to do, but his own father was against this covenant. He tried to manipulate his son's emotions to take Saul's side. When that did not work, he allowed his own anger to control him and attempted to kill his own son. People live out their agenda rather than God's call and God's concern by manipulating people.

Emotional manipulation can be an issue of Satan's schemes to influence us. In 2 Corinthians 2:10-11 Paul tells us Satan manipulates our emotions so we will not forgive people. In Mark 14:55-56 one of his schemes is character assassination. If someone gets caught up in assassinating another person's character you know that Satan is always involved in what is happening. That's the way Satan's strategy works. Know that if you start tearing down somebody else, whether in your own heart or while talking to somebody else, it is not God. If somebody comes to you to talk about someone else, sharing things that do not build that person up, you need to recognize that this is called character assassination and it is not from God. We should stop this spiritual attack by simply saying "Wait, we should not go there. We should be building others up instead of tearing them down."

We do not have to condemn the other person by pointing our finger at them and calling them a sinner or some other name. The reason we should not do that is because all of us have done the same thing at some point in our lives. We should be helping each other break this destructive habit pattern that is fed by the enemy of our soul. So rather than try to pull the sliver out of someone else's eye before we pull the log out of our own eye, we should begin ending this type of habit pattern by simply stopping the conversation.

Another one of Satan's schemes is misdirecting the truth. It is seen when someone tells you just enough of the truth to get you to agree with them but do not tell you the whole story. Genesis 3:1-5 is the account of how Eve was tempted by Satan as he stirred up doubt in Eve's heart. Doubt is an emotion. One of the first spiritual attacks that come against us is to stir up doubt so we no longer trust God and how good He is. So we do not trust how God will take care of us and provide for us. Then Satan will attempt to stir up the emotion of doubt to cause us to doubt other people.

In Ephesians 6:14 we are told that our struggle is not against flesh and blood, (other people), but against spiritual rulers of darkness who manipulate humans to disobey God. They work at twisting our emotions so we do not do what God wants. When they are successful, we have made a commitment not to do what God wants. While we feel like we have not made a commitment to disobey God, we usually justify it by saying that we made a commitment to do something else. But in choosing not to do what God wants we have just chosen not to obey. It really is that simple, we do what God wants or we do not do what God wants.

It is amazing how many people know what God wants them to do, but they do not do it. No matter how big it is, or how small it is – by their own testimony they choose not to do it. Some do not feel worthy to do what God wants them to do while others simply do not trust God that He will provide and take care of them in order to do what He wants or has asked them to do. It is just an issue of obeying God; it is what we are called to do. What you are called to do may look completely different than what someone else is called to do. Comparing ourselves with others is just another way the enemy may use to manipulate our emotions into thinking we should not be the one to obey God.

Now it may be you have noticed when people do what God wants them to do, God will give them more assignments. Have you noticed that about God? If you do what He tells you to do, He is going to ask you, or tell you, to do something else. That is one way to describe it. The Bible says if you are faithful in little things then He will give you greater things. But if you do not want to do things for God, He might not give you other assignments until you finish the last one. Like what happened to Jonah when he did not want to do the assignment given to him.

Here is one of the problems with not doing what God wants. The result is that people do not feel worthy, and the enemy uses shame and guilt to manipulate people by using their feelings of unworthiness to convince them to continue to do little or nothing for God's Kingdom. So when someone else asks you to do something different than what God wants, you may agree to do it, hoping it appeases God. Hoping that maybe you might be able to work your way up to what God has asked you to do, or you try to exchange what God wants with what someone else wants you to do. You have to know and believe that whatever God asks you to do He will give you the strength, the wisdom, and the knowledge as well as surround you with the people to do it.

Watch for the following six ways you can overcome the manipulation of emotions syndrome.

1. Recognize the strategies that are being used. If you do not want to be manipulated emotionally anymore, recognize the strategies being used to manipulate you. When someone tries to guilt you into doing something you need to recognize it as a manipulative strategy. When you are struggling with your emotions over a response someone is looking for, recognize it as something you should not have to struggle with. If your emotional response is "I know this is something God wants me to do", then stop right there. But if someone is trying to guilt you into doing something that you are not sure you are suppose to do, tell them, "Colossians 3:15 says, 'let the peace of Christ rule in your heart.' So I need to wait on God until I have peace about this."

   Do not use this verse as an excuse for not doing what God has told you to do. There are believers in Jesus who know God wants them to obey Him yet because they do not have peace they will not do what God wants. It usually means that they have questions about how it is going to get done, because God has told them what to do.

2. Stay open to Holy Spirit and what God wants of you. Listen for Holy Spirit; seek Holy Spirit's guidance through prayer. Go to other people for counsel and confirmation. I am a person of deep emotions and I have found the most effective person to tell me to step back and take a breath is my wife, because I am the type of person who when I decide to do it . . . boom – we are doing it. She has to say "Hold it,

come back here and let's talk about it. Should we talk about this a little? Might there be another way that we could do this?" Fortunately she is often correct. Look for others who are spiritually mature and share with them, "this is what I believe God wants me to do, what do you think? Is it okay?" But always stay open to Holy Spirit.

3.  When someone's emotions are controlling their response or their reaction and they are trying to get you to agree, because of how they are using their emotions be very cautious. You may be manipulated into giving into what they want. If someone is emotional, step back, take a deep breath and ask God what He wants you to do, how He wants you to do it.

4.  Look out for those who try to cross over your established boundaries. Choose not to give into others manipulation through using established boundaries you refuse to let others cross. If anyone says "I have to know right now" you should have set a boundary that requires you will at least consult Holy Spirit before saying yes. There are times you will know immediately what God wants you to do because of your relationship with Him. Yet be sure that any pressure to give an answer immediately is not a strategy for manipulating your emotions. At least be willing to take a couple of minutes to seek God.

    Believers in Jesus Christ do not need to fast and pray for the answer to every request. If we have said to God "I will do whatever you want me to do". When He presents us the opportunity to minister, we should not need to fast and pray for 30 days to come up with an answer. We should be able to stop and simply ask, "Lord, what do you want me to do." If God's Spirit says "Yes or No" then you have your answer.

Since Holy Spirit was given to us to guide and lead us, that is exactly what He will do. Your answer may be "I am sensing this may be something I should do, but I believe I need to seek God a little longer – let me get back to you."

Remember that boundaries are not walls. There are times that our boundaries are set, yet God may tell us to go outside the boundaries. This is why we need to be close enough to God so we know the difference between Him telling us to go outside the boundary and our emotions stirring us to think "That poor person, I should help them" when God is saying "Don't help them."

5. Train your spirit to recognize the difference between your emotions and Holy Spirit's voice. If you do not feel you hear well from God, surround yourself with people who do, pray with people who do. You can learn from them. Sometimes by watching them. Sometimes by asking them about how they learned, or what they just experienced. Ask them questions like "How did you know that God was speaking to you? What did it sound like?" You need to train your spiritual ears to know when Holy Spirit says "Go and do this."

6. Remember that emotions are the easiest area to control and manipulate in our lives. Our emotions are easily controlled and manipulated by ourselves (by our flesh and what it wants), by other people and by the enemy. Throughout Scripture and life – pride, anger, fear, and lust for more – are used spiritually to control people and influence spiritual matters, both for the Kingdom of Light and darkness. God can use your emotions to get you to do what He wants you to do. The enemy can use your emotions to get you to do what the enemy wants.

How do you know the difference? You have to know God, and that is something no one else can do for you. You have to know God. It has been said many times by many people, "Everyone has as much of God as they want." For in knowing God you will know His voice and recognize His leadings.

Spiritual people are influenced all the time. At times by God through Holy Spirit for His Kingdom, or by others who have learned the way of the enemy. People who have learned how to manipulate, as a strategy of the enemy, can come to spiritual people and make them think that what they are doing is what God wants. It is why each of us has to set boundaries and establish the answer to what does God want you to do.

When someone comes to a pastor and says "You need to do this because you are the pastor", the pastor should say "No, the Bible says 'You are the ministers' so I will put you in touch with someone from the congregation who may help you." Pastors cannot do everything people want, no matter how others play their emotional cards. There are life circumstances that people in the congregation have experienced which the pastor has not, so they are better equipped to help another person through their situation. That would make them a source of encouragement far greater than the pastor ever could if they are willing to step up and tell God "Yes, I'll let your Spirit lead me in that way."

When your emotions rise up in a decision making process always ask yourself eight words, "Is this what God wants me to do." If you ask, "What would Jesus do?" there are many things Jesus would do that most people are not willing to do. It is not that we are not able to do it; we just use the excuse

– "that's what Jesus would do". If you ask "God is this what you want me to do?" and He says "Yes", then you can ask "What would Jesus do?" because that is what you need to step into and do yourself. This way when you are ministering to someone you will not feel manipulated in what you are doing. Instead you will be able to know that God has given you this responsibility.

Watch today for the manipulation of people's emotions. It happens often. It happens to those around you. Don't give into it because either you control your emotions, or your emotions will control you.

## Chapter 12

# The "It's My Parent's and Society's Fault" Disorder

Take a moment and think of yourself as having a "chooser switch" inside you. What's a chooser switch? It's the switch you flip inside you, one way or the other, when you make a choice. "Yes I'll do this, no I won't." Picture that switch inside you, it will look different for each of us. When you heart makes a decision and your mind agrees, you flip a switch and you choose to do one thing or the other. With it you choose to do what's right or what's wrong. It's a switch that nobody can switch . . . but you, because it is inside you alone.

There is a switch on the bedroom wall that anybody could walk over and when flipping it can cause the light to go off. A family member could walk into the room and switch the light on and a friend could walk over and the flip the switch causing the light to turn off. Yet inside you, you alone have your own chooser switch in which you make a choice, no matter what it is you are doing. Nobody else can flip that switch for you. We can blame it on other people by thinking or saying, "It wasn't my fault."

When I was younger there was a house being built up on the corner. In order to put in a septic tank the builder had dug a large hole leaving what looked like a huge mound of soft dirt to a six or seven year old. For those of us who have had the experience of a dirt clod fight at a young age it is a well know fact that the soft dirt makes the best throwing clods as they don't hurt too much when they hit the target. My brother was planning a sneak attack through the house which was not very far along in its construction. Then I spotted him. My brother was looking at me through an open window. I threw a nice dirt clod at him, missing the open part of the window and breaking both the fixed window's glass as well as the sliding portion of the window's glass. Using a warped thought pattern I felt it was not my fault, my brother made me throw the dirt clod at him . . . and some would say it was probably my parent's fault for not keeping better track of what her children were doing. Or so the thought pattern would lead us to think. In reality, it was my fault – I chose to throw the dirt clod.

The reality is while people may influence which way you flip the switch, you ultimately choose what you do. Nobody chooses it for you. In our society we are often so messed up about the responsibility for taking action. When someone chooses to do something wrong our society responds emotionally with a rationale that says "It wasn't their fault." Another person responds with "Yeah, but they did it." And the response is "But it wasn't their fault." We might even think it wasn't "my" fault or even it wasn't "anybody's" fault. We do not seem to want people to have to take responsibility for so many of their actions.

Our society looks for people to blame, yet blaming someone is different than taking responsibility for one's actions. A few years ago a professional quarterback in the NFL named Michael Vick was involved as the leader of a dog fighting organization and before anything went to trial he stood in front of the cameras at a press conference to say "I made a mistake." What he did was not a mistake. A mistake is something you do by accident. Taking responsibility for his decisions would have been to say "I did something wrong." There were people at the time who tried to blame his action on his upbringing. They said that where he grew up dog fighting was an acceptable sport in his community. Even now the memory of this portion of his life may be invoking certain feelings within us because as a society we do not want to have people take responsibility for their actions, to recognize that their chooser switch was flipped by them. Instead we want to find a way to blame it on their upbringing, the society they were raised in or often their parents. Again, blaming their action on others rather than having them take responsibility for what they have done.

Before we head too far down this path, please understand that the Bible says people need to take responsibility for what they have done. Yet after they have taken responsibility for what they have done, who shows them mercy? God shows us mercy, when we take responsibility for what we have done by forgiving us, by confessing our sin to Him (1 John 1:9). Who shows mercy to somebody who steps up and takes responsibility for what they have done. Make no mistake, there are consequences for the decisions they make, yet who shows the person mercy?

Why is mercy different all the time? Why can one person say something on talk radio and he or she is kicked off the air, when another person says something just as bad and people just let it go? Who decides when to show mercy and what are the boundaries for mercy that is shown to others?

Do you remember the parable in the Bible of the young man who wanted to take half of what his father owned and went out to spend it on whatever he so chose? We call it the parable of the lost or prodigal son. Think about it though, I believe, it actually is a long parable of the merciful father.

Remember the young man was given half of what the father had, leaving home he messed up his life and when he returned he did not try to blame his dad. Where was his dad? He was waiting, looking for his son to return. When his son came back, having thought through his wrong choices, he wanted to become one of his father's servants. The dad said "No way, you're my son." He took his son, lifted him up, put the ring on his finger, the robe on his back and then threw him a party because he had come back. Who threw the party? The father threw the party.

The story did not end there, the older brother became jealous. He heard from a servant that Dad was throwing a party. They had killed the fatted calf and the older brother would not go into the party. Think about it, who went out to talk to the older son? The father did. It was not primarily about the Prodigal, it was not primarily about the older brother – it was all about the father. Rather than focus on the sons, shift your focus to see this as a story about God and His love for His children. Whether they go off and totally mess their life up or whether they stay and do everything that God wants them to do while being mad about having to stay behind and do it this story was about the merciful father. The older brother was not willing to show any mercy to his returning brother in this parable. He is angry because the younger brother got to go out and squander everything he was given. Then the younger brother was given a party when he returned penniless?

The father had to go out and tell his older son, "My son who was lost, has been found, we have to celebrate." Sometimes this account of the older son is a picture of those who have walked with God a long time, are unwilling to show mercy to those who have walked away from their relationship with God and then after messing up their own life they come back to God. We take the person who has returned to God and put them in front of the Church, have them share their testimony of all the horrible experiences they chose to have and rather than be celebrative with them some sit back and judge them. Some say things like "Well, they knew better than that in the first place. They should never have gone that direction."

While seeing this parable in this way may never have occurred to some before, I have seen people in my years in the Church who look at others who have returned to God from a lifestyle that is messed up instead of rejoicing over the person, they look at the person as the older brother did with the mindset of "Why does he get a party, what about me? What about all these things that I've done for you Dad?" God wants us to enjoy our relationship with Him and to do that we have to enjoy our relationship with each other. That reality sometimes messes us up because we think that we can be upset at other people but be okay with God. Our relationship with each other is supposed to be a picture of our relationship with God. On the one hand we need to talk about people needing to take responsibility for what they do, but we need to be just as quick to extend the mercy when they do take that responsibility.

God's view of who is responsible for what happens in life tends to be different than our society's view. People's emotional responses these days sometimes are to say "Let's just share the blame." My roommate and I were in seminary together while working with the Youth Group from a local congregation and we did not have a bus or van. He owned an older Oldsmobile and was driving on a street that naturally curved to the left. While in the curve another young man in his early twenties missed the corner and hit the side of my roommate's Oldsmobile with his vehicle. No one was hurt. After getting out of their vehicles and while waiting for the police to show up to take their report, the young man said to my roommate, "You know, we were both at fault." My roommate asked "How do you figure? My car was in its lane

. . . ." The other man replied, "You could have swerved to avoid me."

That is an example of how we look for ways to include other people, rather than admitting it is our fault, so we do not have to take the blame. We see that with parents who have multiple children. If one is in trouble they might as well make them all be in trouble. If two children were present often parents will want to know why the one who did not participate in wrongful behavior did not stop the other who was acting wrongly. If the child not participating was the older child they often are blamed for not making the younger one stop because the parents might say "you are the responsible one". This implies that the other should not be held responsible for wrongdoing. Sometimes there are not multiple people responsible, there is only one person responsible and we have to live with that.

In Exodus 20:4-6 in the middle of the second of the 10 commandments the Bible says: "You shall have no other gods before Me. You shall not make for yourself an idol or any likeness of what is in heaven above or on the earth beneath or in the water under the earth. You shall not worship them or serve them; for I, the LORD your God, am a jealous God, visiting the iniquity of the fathers on the children, on the third and the fourth generations of those who hate Me, but showing lovingkindness to thousands, to those who love Me and keep My commandments."

This has been used many times to explain generational sin. An example of generational sin is if your father is an alcoholic you will tend to become an alcoholic. While that is true, the punishment for your father's alcoholism is not that you will be an alcoholic. Also notice that God will visit the sins of the fathers on the third and fourth generations of those who hate God. Remember in the Hebrew the words for hate and love are more about choosing than the emotions we tie to these words in our society. Hate is more about choosing against something, while love is more about choosing for something. So in Exodus 20 God is saying He visits the sin of the fathers on their children to the third and fourth generation of those who do not choose God or hate God.

Let's look again at verse 6: "showing lovingkindness to thousands, to those who love Me and keep My commandments."

So even though the sin of the fathers will be visited on those who hate God, if you love God He says He is going to bless thousands who love Him and keep His commandments. It could accurately be interpreted a thousand generations.

Yet the heart of the issue seems to be that children tend to worship what their parents do. God is saying that if you make an idol that you bow down and worship, your children are probably going to do that as well. What parents give their lives to; many children also give their lives to. That's where the generational sin may be passed down. Yet God's love is so overwhelmingly greater than the visitation of sin that's passed on to the children of parents who teach their children to worship other gods. A child tends to act the way they do because of how their parents acted, but a child is not responsible for their parent's sin. A child is only responsible for their own sin. In the same way a parent is not responsible for a child's sin because, remembering the chooser switch, the child makes the choice not the parent.

Even though we may talk about little children and their parent's influence, the child as they grow up still will make choices. It may be true that children will often mimic what their parents do but it is not always the case. I know of a man who is now in the military. His sister was a prostitute who was murdered. His mom and dad were both alcoholics. His dad and his brother were in and out of jail. Yet at the age of 15 he went down to the police department and turned himself in asking to be placed in a different home. The police officer said to him, "Not everyone has the courage to do that."

225

His life radically changed because he chose to take himself out of this home with such despair and hopelessness and be placed into foster care because he recognized he needed different influences in his life. Last I heard he is a Colonel in the U.S. Army and has made a career out of it. He is an incredible man who at the age of 15 had to make a difficult choice. People say that would be horribly difficult, yet most of us have had to make horribly difficult decisions. Everyone chooses during their life what they do. No one can say all of their life "It wasn't my fault, that's the way my parents raised me."

When you were little you knew it was wrong for someone to take your crayon. Didn't you? No one had to pull you aside and say to you "When they take your crayon away that is wrong." I do not know a single child who when someone takes their toy away says "That's okay." What is the first word it seems a child learns? "MINE!" In so many ways we know what is right and wrong. Romans chapter one says it is built into us to know what is right and what is wrong. So from the very beginning we know whether it is right to do something or it is wrong to do it.

People say that is your conscience. It is also the image of God in us calling us to do what God would do. Today we do not teach people it is their responsibility for what they do, instead we tend to teach them it is not their fault they turned out the way they have. Yet the truth is it is their responsibility as they made the choice they did. Emotionally we do not want people to feel bad about themselves so we blame someone else for what they did.

In Ezekiel 18 God makes this clear. In verses one to four God says that every living soul belongs to Him and the soul who sins will die. In verse 5-9 He talks about people who do what is right in God's eyes and how they will live. In verses 10-13 God talks about a child whose father has done what is right in God's eyes, yet the child does not do what is right in God's eyes is responsible for their sins and their actions. Today we have people who believe that if their child does not do what is right in God's eyes it is totally their parent's fault. It is the responsibility of the child who sins as everybody makes their own choices.

People may say, what about the father who is abusive, isn't there a tendency for the child to be abusive? Yes, we have seen this tendency in people's lives. But the child does not have to be abusive. Jesus can set people free. Jesus can take what looks like it has been passed on generationally and He can stop it at one generation. Jesus can say "That's it. This pattern of sin is not going on any further. This person will not be abusive anymore. This person will not be an alcoholic and their children after them will not be alcoholics."

In verse 14-18 God introduces a third generation. He has talked about a father who does what is right, a son who does what is wrong, and then a grandson who does what is right again. God says that the third generation is not responsible for what the second generation did, whether that is the father or the mother who did not do what God wanted. They are not responsible for that, only for what they do. As you read this you probably are thinking "Well of course that's true."

It is true, but people often do not think or feel that way. We need to realize that people say everybody is not responsible for what they do. Even though sociology and psychology can point toward activity in someone's life and say this is why it happened, it did not have to happen that way. There are people who were abused as children but never abused someone else. They do not have to take that road, they do not have to go down that path, it is a choice they make and if God is in their life He helps them make their choices not to do what has been done to them.

Even those who are not walking with God have the same choice as to whether they are going to follow the same path their parents took or whether they are going to follow a different path. In God's eyes the person responsible is the one who chooses to do whatever they decide to do. Verses 19-20 God says again that the person who sins is the one who dies. In our society we tend to look at a person's life and blame their actions on their parents, the children around them at school or any one of many other factors in their life.

There was a lady a number of years ago who sued McDonalds because she spilled hot coffee in her lap. What the jury said in essence is that "You're not to blame for spilling hot coffee in your lap, McDonalds is." Their decision was that it was not the fault of the lady who bought the hot coffee and spilled it on herself. It was not the fault of person who served her by giving the coffee to her. It was not the fault of the manager for training the server who gave the coffee to her incorrectly. So it must have been the fault of the corporation as a whole, thereby allowing the jury not to have anyone take responsibility for what happened.

The story is told of the man who bought a motor home, set the vehicle on cruise control and then went back to make himself a sandwich because he thought cruise control was like auto pilot. I know a man who works in this field who knows this to be a true story. The man won a lawsuit because there was not sufficient instruction that cruise control was not the same as auto pilot. Our society has so moved to a "this is not your fault mindset' that we tend not to expect people to take responsibility for what they do.

Verses 21-24 in Ezekiel 18 basically say that whether one turns from right or wrong it is the person's decision so in God's eyes they are responsible. If a person who does what is right yet toward the end of their life they choose to walk away from what God wants, they are responsible for that decision. The person who does whatever they want all their life and may mess up seemingly everything they do yet toward the end of their life they change and start doing what is right, God sees that as well. The chooser switch inside each person makes them responsible for their choices one way or the other. Some people believe they keep it in their brain, some believe they keep it in their heart, but each one of us has a chooser switch.

The difference between heart deciders and brain deciders is that the first recognizes that their decisions are tied to their emotions and the second think that they decide based on their intellect which is able to divorce their emotions from their decisions. Yet our emotions impact every decision we make in one way or another and that is the point of this book. Our emotions have been raised to such a high level that we exalt them above just about everything else; even above what God says is right or wrong. We say "If that's the way you feel then that is what you should do."

In verses 25-29 God points out that the house of Israel is arguing with Him. "Yet you say the way of the Lord is not right." Does that not sound like our society?

"Yet you say, ' The way of the Lord is not right.' Hear now, O house of Israel! Is My way not right? Is it not your ways that are not right? When a righteous man turns away from his righteousness, commits iniquity and dies because of it, for his iniquity which he has committed he will die.

"Again, when a wicked man turns away from his wickedness which he has committed and practices justice and righteousness, he will save his life. Because he considered and turned away from all his transgressions which he had committed, he shall surely live; he shall not die. But the house of Israel says, 'The way of the Lord is not right.' Are My ways not right, O house of Israel? Is it not your ways that are not right?"

They were saying "It's not right God, that people should be held responsible for their own decisions, that their choice to turn from their wicked ways is all it takes for them to move into a right relationship with You."

The last three verses are about turning back to God, thinking differently because if you think differently you will act differently. If you think about a decision the way God wants you to, you will most likely do what God wants you to do. But if you think about a decision in a way that is not how God wants you to, you will most likely not do what God wants. I spoke with a lady who was in a Sociology class and the teacher had said, "If you will just act differently than your thoughts will follow." We can act differently but that does that mean our thoughts will follow? We hear about and see people who say or do one thing in order to set people up to think they are someone they are not. Their thoughts and plans are to accomplish something contrary to what they have been doing. For even though they acted one way, later you find it was not the way they were thinking.

But look at verse 30-32. "Therefore I will judge you, O house of Israel, each according to his conduct," declares the Lord GOD. "Repent and turn away from all your transgressions, so that iniquity may not become a stumbling block to you. Cast away from you all your transgressions which you have committed and make yourselves a new heart and a new spirit! For why will you die, O house of Israel? For I have no pleasure in the death of anyone who dies," declares the Lord GOD. "Therefore, repent and live."

The phrase "so the iniquity may not become a stumbling block to you" is a picture of walking down a path and whether you notice it or not beforehand, something in the path makes you stumble. Rather than continue to stumble by doing what God does not want us to do, God will give us a new heart and a new spirit. If your heart and spirit are so prone to sin you may go to God and let Him create in you a new heart and a new spirit. This will transform you to align with God's Spirit in order that you may do what pleases Him.

In Ezekiel 11 God has been speaking to Israel already about the issues of their heart and their spirit. The Lord has talked about gathering them back from the nations and bringing them back from the countries where He has sent them and then God says:

"And I will give them one heart, and put a new spirit within them. And I will take the heart of stone out of their flesh and give them a heart of flesh, that they may walk in My statutes and keep My ordinances and do them. Then they will be My people, and I shall be their God. But as for those whose hearts go after their detestable things and abominations, I will bring their conduct down on their heads," declares the Lord GOD.

Do you realize that if you get to a point where you recognize that your heart or your spirit needs to be transformed, ask God to do that in you. There was a time while praying with a lady at the altar about an issue of her heart God showed her a vision of taking out of her a heart of rock and placing a new heart of flesh inside her. She had no idea God had talked about doing such a thing in the Bible, she had asked Him to help her and He showed her the answer to her prayer.

God does that for us by taking a heart that is wounded or bound up with wrong choices – that is like a rock because it does not care about God at all and in His mercy He takes out the heart of rock saying "This is not any good for you, let me put this heart inside you instead." All of a sudden our heart is transformed and begins to beat with the passion for God that we are supposed to have. So if your heart or spirit is crushed or broken, ask God for a new one and let Him transform the heart and spirit you have that is crushed in that way.

Everyone has opportunities to make the right choices. Some people turn out good, some people turn out bad even though they have had similar upbringings. One of the reasons I believe this is true is because they just do not know God. Another reason is most people lack control of their emotions. They are allowed as they grow up to let their emotions run wild, no one trains them to control their emotions and the result is they do not take responsibility for their choices and actions because no one has trained them. We tend to know that when we make some people take responsibility for their emotions, choices and actions it will make them angry and things will probably become worse.

There was a lady once who the Lord had told to go and share some truth with another woman. Weeks later we were talking and I asked if she ever took the opportunity to share that truth with the other woman and she said "No." When asked why not she replied "I know if I told her that it would only make things worse so I just chose to avoid it."

I responded: "If God shared that with you, what if God was going to use that in her life to bring transformation to her?"

She said, "I just didn't want to take that chance."

That is an example of rather than helping people learn to accept responsibility and then be there to show mercy, some people tend to step back and let whatever is going to happen take place. In society and the Church we tend to let people off the hook. We will not speak the truth that they need to step up to; instead we wonder why nothing changes. It is why the Church is tending to slide more and more into looking like what society as a whole looks like. You see, responsibility in God's eyes **is** a big deal.

In 2 Corinthians 5 we are told that when we stand before God at the judgment seat we will each receive what is due us for what we have done during our lives whether good or bad. Somehow God will weigh into this the forgiveness of confessed sin and the promise of removing it as far as the east is from the west. Yet since this was written about believers it will be true of our lives one day as well.

We need to take responsibility for our own actions and desires. In the book "Alcoholics Anonymous" in which the twelve steps of recovery are spelled out the most important step is the first step. The individual must admit they have a problem to take responsibility for their problem. A person can do the other eleven steps, but without admitting they have a problem the other eleven steps will not be effective in overcoming alcoholism. Until they have dealt with the fact that they are an alcoholic they will not be able to deal with their problem. Step one is the first action to be taken.

Step one for daily living is taking responsibility for what we do. By admitting what we did, we have taken the first step according to 1 John 1:9. "Lord I confess to you that I did this. What do you want me to do now Lord?" He does not accept excuses, so we must admit what we have done. He does not accept our casting the blame on someone else. When going to someone to admit to having wronged them it is better to admit what was done and ask forgiveness than to just say "I apologize" because all that does is say you are sorry for how they feel. It is more important to take responsibility for the action.

Henry Varley once said that it remains to be seen what God will do with a person who gives themselves up wholly to God. Have you thought much about giving yourself up wholly to God? If we are taking responsibility for what we do, we are walking with Jesus like He wants us to, and are filled with Holy Spirit; that is when we will do amazing things for God's Kingdom. We will do less and less wrong and more and more what God wants. So our focus should be how do we get to the place where we are giving ourselves totally to God?

Rather than get down on ourselves for making a previous commitment to God to read our Bibles more or pray more, and then not reaching those goals after another year of trying, it's time to realize some truth. You are not in the same place you were last year, you have been growing for another year. If you are thinking . . . "but I'm not reading my Bible regularly or, I'm not praying like I want to" – then start today. Yes, start doing today what you have been putting off doing, what you already know you need to do for your relationship with God to grow closer and more intimate. The Bible says if you draw close to God, He will draw close to you. Remember that whatever it is you need to do, you can do that as a person totally surrendered to Jesus Christ.

Everyone still has to live their life each day. Jesus did – He still ate, He still lived His life each day. Everybody has lots to do as part of each day's living. When you are a person totally surrendered to God it means in everything you do, you do it for God's glory and He lives through you. Think about the amazing things that could be done if people just walked closer to Jesus. If we take responsibility for our lives by following God's way for our lives, by reading the Bible, by listening to God, by following the promptings of Holy Spirit in our lives –the Kingdom of Heaven will advance through us.

When someone thinks they just do not have time to do these things they need to realize they do have time. People do what people want to do. That is the issue in everyone's life. People do what people want to do. The reason Jesus came is because human beings could not figure out how to do what God wanted on their own. So Jesus came to show us how to do that. Then Jesus died on a cross for us because even though He set the example for us He knew we still would not be able to figure it out on our own. So Father determined that since Jesus always did what God wanted and He never sinned, Jesus' death would count in place of ours having to die to pay for our sins. The Bible says the payment for sin is death, but the gift of God is eternal life through Jesus Christ our Lord. So because Jesus died, we do not have to spiritually die but can spend eternity with God. In John 17:3 Jesus said that eternal life is knowing God and His Son Jesus Christ. Once anyone receives Jesus' death in place of their own, they begin eternal life because they have begun a relationship with God. Knowing God is what eternal life is all about.

Yet after Jesus died God raised Him from the dead and it is because of this people will also be able to be raised again physically to live a new life with God forever. If you are reading this book and have yet to surrender your life to God, you need to take responsibility for your actions, good or bad by asking God to forgive you and determining to make Jesus Christ the Lord of your life. That means making Him the absolute highest authority in your life for every decision you make.

Once you have come to the place of taking responsibility for your life by surrendering it to Jesus and are walking in His ways there are a couple of questions that you should be asking yourself. "Do you know people who do not have parents or others teaching them to take responsibility for themselves? Who will take the responsibility of teaching them and loving them enough to help them learn how to live?" We should because that is what Jesus did. He was constantly teaching people how they should live. It did not matter how old they were.

We need to become spiritual people who become fathers and mothers, sisters and brothers to help other people. Even to help each other out. When we do a child dedication we ask everyone in our congregation to accept the spiritual family's responsibility of praying for and helping the child as they grow up among us. Yet there are people who are never dedicated as a child that need spiritual brothers and sisters, or even fathers and mothers to come alongside them and help them take responsibility for their lives. If we are in a family relationship based on the family of God, we are able to help each other walk with God due to our covenant relationship.

No matter where you are at spiritually you can help people walk with God and take responsibility for their lives. You never know how much influence you have in someone's life.

There is a woman who was out camping with some friends near a waterfall along the Feather River years ago. These friends had been drinking and decided to take a late night walk along the river which was in a drought condition. They decided to enjoy the mossy rock conditions at the top of the waterfall. As they walked back to camp and collapsed on their sleeping bags one of the young men sat up and said to her, "You're a Christian and God does not like your behavior at all, you need to repent." Then he passed out. She rededicated her life and woke the next morning to find that they had been walking about 4 feet from the edge of the waterfall. The Lord made it clear to her that her life was not her own but belonged to Him. God used a drunk young man to make it clear to her that she needed to get right with God.

Think of the impact you can have in people's lives when you are not drunk. If somebody wants to seek help, how should your pastor or leaders help them? They should be hooking these people up with you. You have a life story, you love God and you have much more to offer others than you probably think. People are looking for someone who has gone through what they have gone through and have come out okay.

Jesus helps people in these three ways. First, Jesus helps people when they realize they need Him. You cannot help people who do not want to be helped. You can chase them down, go after them over and over, but if they do not want to be helped, nothing will change. They will remember your love, they will remember you reached out for them but their life will not change until they come to the place where they realize they need and want to be helped. Jesus can step into their life bringing instant change when they will realize they need Him. It can be through the words of another individual or even through a vision of Himself speaking to them.

Second, if someone wants to be helped you need to learn to speak the truth to them in love. Do not tell them that it is not their responsibility, that it's not their fault, that they are not to blame. Speak the truth to them in love. If they were abused, you need to tell them that was not their fault yet what they do now with what has happened to them is their responsibility. It is hard for someone to forgive someone who has done something to them, yet that is always the starting place for their life, because just like God forgives us, we have to forgive other people (Mt 6:14-15).

You need to ask them who they need to forgive. If they say "No one," then just wait on God to reveal the person to them or to you. In order for a lot of the anguish or bitterness of soul to be released people have to forgive others. Sometimes it is themselves they need to forgive. They may have to start by saying "In Jesus name I forgive this person." Then Jesus begins to start a work in their life.

Third, if they do not want to be helped, love them anyway. Care about them, pray for them, be kind to them, do what Jesus did and still does for people by caring and loving them so that at some point God will open the door into that person's life. Then if they ask you why you are doing these things for them you can tell them it's because God loves them and wants to help them. Then they can learn to take responsibility for their life, the things they are doing and the things they have done.

# Chapter 13

# The "You're Not One of Us" Syndrome

When I was in Jr. High I knew a girl and a guy who met in an 8th grade algebra class and developed a crush on each other. She was a nice young lady who was not a Christian, but he was. Within a week of starting to "go out' they broke up as often happens in young relationships. The reason they broke up was he thought their two worlds were too different. Her friends did not see them as being together and his friends did not know about their friendship. Her friends really were not his friends, his friends really were not her friends so they did not seem "to fit" with her group or friends or "to fit" with his group either. They knew each other because they went to the same school, yet it was kind of awkward – they were 13 at the time.

Three years later our Youth Group had a Christmas Banquet. For a number of years the youth of our local congregation would get dressed up for it, kind of like a formal dance, the guys would wear coats and ties, the girls would wear either long dresses or shorter nice dresses. We would have a nice meal and then a Christian entertainer or speaker of some kind would share. We would have a great time. It was fun, it was a safe place for many of our friends to come and many of our Youth Group went on their "first date" with friends at the annual Christmas Banquet. It was a good place to bring friends and have a safe, fun time.

This young man invited the young lady he had a crush on in 8th grade as they had remained friends. She said yes and there was the awkwardness of picking her up, pinning the corsage on, trying to pin the boutonniere on without breaking the stem so the flower wouldn't hang on the lapel of his jacket, and they had a fun time. On the way to and from the banquet they talked, they laughed, they were 16 years old. This was the only time they had ever gone out together.

But something different went on at the banquet that I did not understand until sometime later. After High School and College, when she had grown up and married, had children of her own, we shared a phone conversation. It turned out that at the banquet his friends, who really were still not her friends, made the situation uncomfortable. While her friends did not understand them going out because they viewed the two as so different from each other, the problem at the banquet was that she was not "one of us". While no one said anything she recognized that they felt something was wrong due to her not feeling welcomed. She just did not "fit". Even more than being accepted, she felt she did not fit with his friends. His friends did not allow her to fit in our world because they viewed her as different than "us". She was aware of it, she recognized it but he did not realize it. She recognized this even as a High Schooler.

His friends did not do things to deliberately make her feel uncomfortable. They did not say things to her that would have caused her to think she did not fit. She just did not experience acceptance from them from the time she walked in. She just knew, she sensed, she did not fit in our lives, into our church setting, into our friendships. She did not have the impression that she fit just as he did not have the impression he fit into her group of friends.

You can walk into a room and know whether you fit. When people go to office parties, even family occasions they know when they walk into the room that there is a group over here that they will not spend much time with because they do not fit. They are not going to try to make other people fit. Then there are other people who even though they are not good friends with the person, are able to help the person fit into their group.

This young lady did not fit at the banquet. She had no impression that she fit, even as he knew he would not fit into some of the events in her life. It was okay that he did not fit into some of those expectations that her friends who had broken lives shared because at that point he did not recognize that their lives were broken. Often in Jr. High and High School you see things that are going on in other people's lives without recognizing those things as brokenness in somebody else's life. You know they are going through a difficult time but do not call it brokenness. We do not usually call it brokenness until we get older and look back on it realizing, "Boy when I was in High School . . . . It was just, whew . . . a tough time."

But here's the point. It was not and is not okay that she sensed she did not fit or feel welcomed into the Christian lifestyle that this young man and others shared. He may have feared what her friends thought of him, he was taught to fear them. Her friends as well as their thoughts, he was taught to be afraid of. But what she experienced, she would never have experienced with Jesus Christ. Jesus did not judge others by presuppositions, by doctrines or even by their lifestyles. With Jesus there was not a "you're not one of us" mindset, syndrome or even a disorder. It is something we have learned.

We were a lot younger then. We were taught to fear and avoid friendship with people who did not believe like we believed, even other Christians. We were of one denominational persuasion, and there were other denominational persuasions that are going to be in heaven because they have surrendered their lives to Jesus Christ, but because they did not believe like we believed we were taught they were wrong. We were taught to be afraid of them, that they were wrong. Since they were wrong, implied was fear them, have little or nothing to do with them or they might mislead you too. We were not taught to treat people like Jesus treated people. But we thought we were doing what God wanted. We believed we were doing what God wanted. Yet these excuses for poor behavior, behavior and attitudes that God does not want us to have toward other people whether they are believers or not, are just poor excuses.

Jesus lived to meet people where they were at. Their clothes did not matter to Him. Their hairstyle did not matter to Him. How they lived and what they looked like did not keep them from being loved by Jesus. Not even their language or their abusive language – there were probably people who cussed around Him – did not keep them from being accepted and loved by Jesus. Because Jesus always allowed people to sense that they fit where ever He was.

He did not change who He was to make them feel comfortable. He just loved them in the midst of who He was. The Son of God who came to save the world, made everyone who came to Him feel like they fit. John 3:17 says God did not send His Son into the world to condemn the world but that the world might be saved through Him. Jesus came to draw people to Father God, not condemn them by not allowing them to fit with Him.

No one has to have believed in Jesus to have been touched by the "You're not one of us Syndrome". Anyone who has experienced Jr. High and High School is able to think of a time when they walked up to a group of students at school and felt the "you're not one of us syndrome." You may even have experienced that in Elementary School or even in your work place today.

The religious leaders of Jesus' time saw Him meeting with tax collectors and sinners, which is often put in quotation marks because they were looked down on as disreputable people. The religious leaders judged them, and judged Jesus for being with them because they judged the people first. So they missed the simple fact that these were people who needed God. These religious leaders would look down on others because they were not going to "fit" with the religious leaders. They were held captive by the "You're not one of us Syndrome."

But these people who did not fit with their framework in their day were still loved by God, just not by the religious leaders and sometimes by each other. People of God, it is a bad thing that we have been taught and may have done that causes people to feel they do not fit with us. Where ever we go, if we cause someone to feel they do not fit, they cannot fit, there is something wrong. That is not what Jesus did and we say we want to be like Jesus. It is bad because it was and still is not something that Jesus would ever do to someone. He saw and continues to see everyone through His eyes of compassion and mercy, while He wants everyone to come to know Father God, He knows that making others feel like they do not fit with His own people is not right.

There are two truths that we need to embrace as followers of Jesus Christ. ***The first is that people are looking for love, acceptance and forgiveness.*** Remember in Jesus' day that most people did not fit with the Religious Leaders and what they were teaching. They were able to discern that they did not fit because those who should have known better treated them in a way that said "You don't belong with us." Unfortunately for Christians, that's how we often treat others. They do things that Christians are not supposed to do because they are people who do not believe in Jesus. The emotional response of most people in Jesus' day was to turn away in rejection and feel condemnation from the Religious Leaders. While we agree that this was their choice by embracing their own emotions, the point is simply that Jesus wants us to treat other people as He did and does. Jesus treats everyone with love, acceptance and forgiveness, even when they do not seem to us to fit.

In John 8 we find Jesus came to the temple courts where all the people were gathering around Him so He sat down to teach them. The teachers of the law brought in a woman who they said was caught in the act of adultery. There was no concern of what this said to this woman or about this woman, or what others thought. Their point was to put Jesus on the spot at her expense and they did not care what everyone else would think, whether it would be true or not. They made her stand before Jesus and this group of people and put Jesus on the spot at her expense. They spoke of what the Law of Moses commanded – that she be stoned to death. Then questioned Jesus accusatively and wanted to know "What do you say?" You may know the story, how Jesus bent down and began writing on the ground with His finger.

This was not something they asked Him once or twice, they just kept going after Jesus and yet He continued to write in the ground. Finally He stood up and said "If any of you is without sin, let him be the first to throw a stone at her." Then he stooped down and started writing in the ground again. Each of these teachers of the law began to walk away, the oldest first until only Jesus was left with the woman still standing there. Jesus stood up and looked her in the eyes. He asked her where everyone had gone. Asking was there no one left who had been condemning her? She replied "No one sir."

His response to her was "Neither do I condemn you, go now and leave your life of sin."

What a great example, the Religious Leaders probably thought, there was no way that she could fit into Jesus world. She was caught in adultery. She did not fit who they saw as someone who was worthy of God's love, only their condemnation. They were using her to get to Jesus. They did not even care about her or the consistency of their own beliefs. If you wonder what is meant by the consistency of their own beliefs – ask yourself: "Where was the man?" If the woman was caught in adultery there had to be a man involved. We smile and agree – "Yeah, yeah that's true!" But how different is it today? Would you follow me with this thought for a paragraph?

When talking with people who are working to rid the United States of human trafficking, especially of prostitution, if you ask them "Is it true in cases of prostitution that most of the time the man involved isn't even charged, but only the woman?" you will find the answer to be "Yes". Typically if anything is going to happen to the perpetrator (or the man), he is required to go to classes for about two hours where a former prostitute and others come to speak to him about prostitution. But it's not typically effective because there are not legal ramifications to punish the man. The women however, get thrown in jail or juvenile hall, depending on their age. I find that interesting because this issue has not changed since Jesus' day. What about the man who was, who is involved?

Think about what happened in the account of John 8. Jesus knew what the Religious Leaders wanted. They wanted to stone her and He conditionally gave them permission. When they were not able to meet the condition of not having sinned, they left. Do you see the genius in that? They were saying they wanted to stone her. Jesus said "OK, whoever has not sinned, you through the first stone at her and then everyone else can join in." He gave them exactly what they wanted but they could not do it because the first one to throw a stone would have a problem. Everyone would turn on that man and say "You're a liar!" and go after him. There was enough recognition of what was right there, that they walked away. And Jesus, who still could have condemned her Himself because He was without sin, chose not to condemn her either. Yet Jesus did not let her off the hook, He told her to go and change her lifestyle of sin.

Let's get practical for a minute. If you know a prostitute or someone who is living in adultery, how do you treat them? Do you treat them like Jesus would? And if you say "I don't know any prostitutes." Do you know anybody who is living in adultery, or committed adultery? How do you treat them? There are local congregations where if a young couple have sex they make them come before the congregation and confess their sin. IF that is a requirement for the forgiveness of sin why doesn't everyone who has sex outside of marriage, or who lies, have to stand before the congregation and confess their sin? Why is that a worse sin than other things we do? Why do we condemn people for some sin and not for others? A deeper question is "Why didn't Jesus? Why have we lowered the bar to make some things worse sins than other things?" What about stealing? What about people who cannot handle their anger and it gets out of control? What about people who slander or gossip about other people? Or anything that doesn't show God's love – what about that? Shouldn't we treat everyone the same way? This is being asked in the context of "Did Jesus make the woman stand in front of the Temple Court to tell everybody present that she was wrong?" The answer of course is "No." The issue is *shouldn't we treat people like Jesus did?*

What if someone is living in sin? Then just like Jesus, we should go to them in love, not letting them continue in the sin without accountability. But we should go to them

246

to restore them. In Luke 19:1-10 is the story of Zaccheus. When Jesus came to town Zaccheus wanted to see Him so Zaccheus climbed into a Sycamore tree to get a look. He was a chief tax collector and the tax collectors were not liked by the people of their time. Add to that he was short and most people's level of respect for an adult was probably not raised when they saw him climbing up in a tree. Jesus chose him out of the tree by calling him by name and inviting Himself to Zaccheus' house as the place Jesus was going to stay.

What did the people do? They complained and grumbled because Jesus was going to his house to stay and to eat with him. You see in their eyes Zaccheus was a "sinner." Now doesn't it make sense that whoever's house Jesus would stay in was a "sinner?" The thought must have been that Zaccheus happened to be a worse sinner than "I am." Wouldn't that be called pride?

What ended up happening because Jesus found a way to make Zaccheus fit into Jesus' world was that Zaccheus recognized he was a sinner, without Jesus having to preach at him? Zaccheus declared that he would give half of his possessions to the poor and if he had defrauded anyone of anything, he was going to give back four times as much. He turned from his evil ways, gave back to people what he had taken from them and it happened all because Jesus knew how to make him fit. Do you see how Jesus made him fit? He said "I love you so much that I want to eat your food." This could be a new ministry line for some people.

Do you know why Zaccheus responded as he did? People treated him so poorly that for Jesus to initiate a relationship with him by calling him out in front of everybody who had lined the streets to see Jesus, it allowed his eyes to be open to the love, acceptance and forgiveness Jesus offered. This is a man everyone else would reject and Jesus called him out in front of all of them. Jesus went to be with him. People are looking for love, acceptance and forgiveness and when we live in a lifestyle syndrome that tells others "You're not one of us", we just push them away from God. We are God's representatives here on earth. So what others see in us and how we treat people is exactly what they should expect from God. That means that we should be saying to ourselves, "Everybody should expect me to treat them the way Jesus would if I want to be like Jesus."

*The second truth we need to realize is that people who call themselves followers of Jesus Christ should not have the "You're not one of us syndrome" with each other.* If this strikes a chord in your heart, please take it personally as Holy Spirit stirs within you this truth. It's true for all of the Body of Jesus Christ, not just for an individual local congregation. In Mark 9 the disciples were always trying to learn from Jesus. They were committed followers of Jesus, that is what a disciple is, and they wanted to be like Him. Yet in verse 38 John said to Jesus "Teacher, we saw someone casting out demons in Your name, and we tried to prevent him because he was not following us." He was saying "He wasn't one of us!" and Jesus' response was classic.

"Do not hinder him, for there is no one who will perform a miracle in My name, and be able soon afterward to speak evil of Me. For he who is not against us is for us."

Do you see that? Do you get what Jesus is saying? In this passage Jesus tells them that if someone is not against us, they are for us. Jesus was saying that if people are driving out demons or doing a miracle in "My name", then that person is not against us, but is for us. Jesus never intended for those of us who call ourselves His followers to be as divided as we are today. To use "You're not one of us" with anyone who is a follower of Jesus Christ, is just not right. There are Conservative Evangelicals who live out the "You're not one of us mindset" when they say "We'll worship with you as long as you do it our way. If you start doing it your way among us, we won't accept you." There was a lady who came to me one day and said "You're raising your hands too high, it's distracting me in my worship." What she was really saying was "I'm not comfortable with lifting my hands, so you shouldn't lift your hands."

There are Charismatic and Pentecostals who live out the "You're not one of us mindset" when they say "We won't pray with you or worship with you unless you let us do it our way." We have to realize there are different streams that flow into the river of God and just because one stream does not look like the stream we are in does not make the stream wrong. It doesn't mean we are to tell those that flow in that stream that they are not "one of us."

There are also Christians who say "You make us feel unworthy when you talk about what God has done in your life and we have not experienced it ourselves. You are just trying to make me feel unworthy." No, that's not the case, but the "You're not one of us mindset" tries to wriggle its way in to divide us from each other. When someone either says "As soon as you start to experience God in this way . . . you're no longer one of us" or "If you don't experience God in this way . . . you're not one of us" we are negating what Jesus spoke in Mark 9:39. Do you understand the inconsistency in saying these things?

It is heard when someone says "We have the right to speak in tongues when we are with you. Because you aren't Spirit-filled like we are, you don't fit." Jesus doesn't say anywhere in the Gospels those kinds of words to people. When the Church of Jesus Christ comes together, and those present are committed followers of Jesus – we need to get over those differences. Whether we practice all of the spiritual gifts in 1 Corinthians 12 or whether we only practice some of them – there is a common bond that holds us together. His name is Jesus Christ and as His followers we need to embrace each other. As people who embrace signs, wonders and miracles we need to find ways to embrace brothers and sisters in the

Lord and will be in heaven with us, who do not embrace this type of move of God.

When Jesus said in John 17 that we would be one as He and Father God is one. It meant that when we do not agree on something doctrinally, we still have to embrace each other anyway if we are going to be like Jesus because we have the same Father God.

My brother and I are both ministers who believe some things that are spiritually different. Still we are brothers, both biologically and spiritually, and will be spending eternity in heaven. We have a dysfunctional mindset in the Church today. Consider your own family. Even if a member in your family does something strange or illegal, they are still your family. Just as we did not get to vote on who is in our biological family, neither do we get to vote on who is in God's family. God wants the people who are in His family to fit together. If they choose not to fit with us, then that is their choice, but we need to do everything we can to help each other fit together.

There are those who teach people that if someone doesn't pray as they do, worship as they do, act as they do or believe exactly as they do, that person is to be rejected or at least feared because they are dangerous to be around. They teach that because people respond differently to God – on each end of the scale. Yet that was not the mindset of Jesus Christ. If someone believes differently, worships differently or uses a different version of the Bible than you do, if Jesus Christ is their Lord then they should be loved, accepted and forgiven just like they should treat you. If they do not treat you that way, it should not matter to you because Jesus loved, accepted and asked Father God to forgive people whether they loved and accepted Him or not. This is an issue that also has to cross racial lines. What ever race a believer is should not exclude them from being loved and accepted by brothers and sisters of another race. Our focus should not be on our race

250

or our culture but on our Lord Jesus. He is supposed to be our focus – nothing else should stand in His way. As people of different races, we need to embrace each other. Jesus was a Jewish man – how can we embrace Jesus and not embrace brothers and sisters of other races.

What we will see in the coming years because God has been reestablishing the apostolic and prophetic ministries spoken of in Ephesians 4:11-13 is that some denominations will initially reject them. The reason will be they are concerned that if there are apostolic and prophetic ministries speaking into local congregations, some of these congregations will move in the direction Holy Spirit is directing instead of the direction the denominations are heading. Because those denominations are afraid of these terms found in the Bible, they will not be willing to embrace them. They will go even further than not embracing them. They will determine if you choose to believe that the first two ministries of the five ministries listed that were established in the New Testament are for today, "you are not one of us."

Jesus wants our mindset to be that everyone should be able to fit. They may not become your closest friend but everybody should fit in the body of Christ. When someone new is introduced and the conversation starts up, as you find something out about whom they are and what they do, it should trigger within you people they can relate to in the congregation you attend. When they find someone they have something in common with, often they will feel like they fit.

The way we begin to get out of the "You're not one of us syndrome" is first to ask God to open our eyes to see people the way Jesus does. As soon as we see people the way Jesus does we will not forget them. Holy Spirit will bring to mind what He told you about them. It may be "That's the person who is touching children's lives by being a school bus driver.

That's the business leader who is touching co-workers lives by being a servant leader at work."

Secondly, talk with people. Make the effort to go to someone you do not know and start a conversation with them. If you believe that you are not the type of person who can do this, you need to find some people to pray with you to be delivered from that mindset because God does not intend for you to believe that way. He intends for you to take His glory, His promises, and His testimonies and share them with other people.

If you are so withdrawn that you are not able to talk with other people God wants to set you free from that. He wants you to be a glowing testimony of what Holy Spirit is doing in your life and in other people's lives. If when you enter a gathering of people and you feel things closing in on you, God wants to set you free from that. It is not how He intended you to live your life. Find someone to pray with you who will not give up asking God for your deliverance until Holy Spirit touches you and brings about the change you are seeking. Then find someone to mentor you in this lifestyle change.

Thirdly, bless people. Everyone you meet, everywhere you go – become a person who blesses others. When we say "God bless you" we are imparting a blessing over others, even when they are too busy to acknowledge our words.

The fourth practical way we get out of this syndrome is to accept people. Romans 15:7 says "Therefore, accept one another, just as Christ also accepted us to the glory of God." This is why we accept others, because Jesus accepted us. Since we want to be like Jesus, we have to accept others.

The fifth way is to remember that Jesus loves you; He loves people and brings others into your life for a reason. He trusts you with that person's life. Go places where other Christians are and practice these things. Go places where people are who do not know Jesus and practice these ways of breaking out of this syndrome. Before you start coming up with all kinds of reasons why you can not, you will not, or you should not choose to participate in these five ways, choose instead to say yes to Jesus asking you to be like Him in your daily life. Go places where you can help others fit into the Kingdom of God. Go places . . . , like where? Anywhere and everywhere you go can be a place where you are able to help others fit into the Kingdom of God. Go to Conferences, go to Prayer Gatherings, go to Special meetings during the week or on the weekend, go to worship somewhere when you are on vacation, go to your local coffee place, go to the grocery store (everybody needs food at some point) – go to meet people and help them fit into the Kingdom of God. Bring other people with you to help them fit. If you will do these things, the people who you bring with you will learn from what you are doing and will begin to do the same.

Take a minute now to tell God you are willing to love, accept and extend forgiveness to people when they show up in your life because you want to recognize them as having been brought by God into your life even as He brought lots of people into Jesus' life. Ask God who He wants you to talk with, to bless, to accept where you go today.

Remember the young lady at the beginning of this chapter. She gave her life to Jesus. It was through the consistent life of her older brother who helped her understand that she does fit in God's Kingdom and she came to know the love, acceptance and forgiveness of Jesus. They met every week for breakfast when they were in their thirties. He would continue to tell her about Jesus and His love until she gave her life to Jesus. She loves Jesus now. Yet I can't help but wonder how many other people I know have not experienced God simply because they have sensed that they did not "fit in" and how much that needs to change. Will you help anybody and everybody fit with God?

Rather than feel guilty about the people in the past who have not felt they fit, tell the Lord from this point on you want to practice these ways to help people fit. If He brings someone from your past to mind – do your best to look up the person and see if they have found out that Jesus wants them to fit in His Kingdom.

# Chapter 14

# The "I want to be like Jesus" Lifestyle

No matter where one is at emotionally, everything keeps coming back to wanting to be like Jesus. For if a person is like Jesus they will know how to control their emotions instead of their emotions controlling them. Jesus was completely correct and controlled in how He used His emotions. He had emotions that were displayed all through the gospels just like Father God has emotions and they are displayed throughout the Bible.

Jesus demonstrated those with the disciples. It is seen over and over as He poured Himself into them. One cannot pour oneself into others without one's emotions impacting them, the passion of who you are and what you want to see Father God do impacting people's lives. The followers, not just the twelve, but everyone else who followed as well, learned from Jesus' emotions. When they were hungry He took care of them. When they were tired emotionally and physically, Jesus was concerned for them. When people needed healing His concern was not going home and going to bed early but it was to stay all through the night at times because of His compassion He had for people.

There were times that people became angry and disappointed and those were their emotions as well. Do you realize disappointment is an emotion? It is something that can be turned around completely since people choose to be disappointed. Sometimes people were harsh, others were trying to mislead them – Jesus was in the midst of all of that and His emotions were always completely under control. I do not know about you but I want to be like Jesus. Father God knew that we could not figure out or discover a great deal of what happens in this life and our future without a relationship with Him. I want to repeat that statement for emphasis. God knew that we could not figure out or discover a great deal of what happens in this life and our future without a relationship with Him. So He decided to help us out by sending His Son as a little baby. Think about it, when Jesus was born people did not fully understand what was going to take place.

A friend of mine named Tony was sharing once how sad it is that we only look at the Christmas story once a year because of how much we could learn from the way God helped the people in the account in Luke 1 to understand what was going to happen in their lives. He sent an angel to explain to them incredible truths so that they would be better able to handle their own emotions in the midst of what God would do. As the narrative unfolded there were prophetic words spoken by Elizabeth and by Mary. In chapter 2 more angels showed up to announce that Jesus the Savior of the world had been born. The excitement of the moment must have been intense. It was a celebration of what God had done and was going to be doing.

It was not the most popular people or the most well known people of the time that the angel was sent to, it was a group of shepherds out watching their sheep at night. What an emotional time for these people plucked out of history to experience the celebration of Father God over His Son, over His plan to open up the possibility of relationships with all who are willing. As one continues through the second chapter of Luke the account of baby Jesus being brought to the temple to be dedicated brings an encounter with a servant of the Most High God coming into Joseph and Mary's lives to bless their new born son. Followed immediately by a prophetess who too had been waiting for just this time, just this child to be brought to the temple for this dedication – what an emotionally high experience everyone involved went through.

Jesus took on the likeness of human beings to display the image of God correctly through a human body and personality. He showed that people are able to know God, be in control of their emotions and lives by being Spirit-filled, while seeing amazing things happen just like Jesus did. I want to be like Jesus. Jesus lived His life to demonstrate to us that we can live our lives with balanced emotions. From being a child all the way to His death on the cross, He was born so all creation would have the opportunity to know God. The entire reason for His coming and living His life was so that you and I could know God. Even the description of the New Covenant in Jeremiah 31 and Hebrews 9 speaks of knowing God. Jeremiah 31 verse 33 says,

"But this is the covenant which I will make with the house of Israel after those days," declares the LORD.

If you think that you are not part of the house of Israel go back and read through Romans and the first 3 chapters of Galatians where believers are taught that we are the seed of Abraham who by faith have become a part of this Covenant and this blessing.

"I will put My law within them and on their heart I will write it; and I will be their God, and they shall be

My people. They will not teach again, each man his neighbor and each man his brother, saying, 'Know the LORD,' for they will all know Me from the least of them to the greatest of them. . ."

Wrapped in the New Covenant is the fact that we need to know God. That He wants us to know Him. The issue will one day be settled when we come to the place of standing before God at the end of our lives as to whether we know God. For that is what will separate those who are allowed to enter into heaven or sent to spend eternity separated from God in Hell. That will be the difference.

In Matthew 7 Jesus explained that there will be people who will have prophesied in His name, cast out demons in His name, and done many miracles in His name yet He will tell them to depart from His presence because He never knew them. It is all about knowing God. By entering into this incredible Covenant, this commitment Father God made to human beings, anyone is able to know God. Think about that – if you have surrendered your life to God you know God. Maybe not to the depth you want, but you have started that relationship which will enable you to know God as deeply as you are willing to pursue Him. It has been said "You have as much of God as you want." You know God as deeply as you have been willing to spend time with Him, to interact with Him, even to follow His ways.

In the end He says: "for I will forgive their iniquity, and their sin I will remember no more."

That forgiveness is based on what Jesus did. In Romans Paul shared about the difference between Adam and Jesus. Adam's actions were based on his emotions and because of those emotional decisions he chose not to do what God wanted. He determined to follow his wife's example and they ate the fruit that God had told them not to eat. But Jesus controlled His emotions when He had more than one opportunity not to. Particularly as Satan tempted Him to short cut the reason He was sent by Father God. Remember how Satan eventually offered Jesus all the kingdoms of the world if He would bow down and worship Satan. Jesus continued to do what Father God wanted even though He had opportunities like this to avoid the cross.

The whole point of Satan offering Jesus so much was to get Jesus to skip the cross. When he offered Jesus all the authority over the kingdoms of the world by just bowing down to him, Jesus said, "I'm not going to do that." Think about it. Jesus did not have to die for us, there were all kinds of other choices He could have made that would have given in to His emotions, but He chose to die for us. What makes that incredible is that the Bible says that Jesus was totally human because He was born of a human mother. So everything you and I are tempted with Jesus was tempted with as well. But He kept choosing what He knew Father God wanted Him to do.

People do not understand that if we would act like Jesus and be like Jesus then we would control our emotions and how we display them to other people. It is when I selfishly use my emotions that I do not do what God wants and I do not treat other people the way God wants me to treat them. As you have read this book does it not amaze you how much emotions affect every single one of us? Either we control our emotions or they control us. There are two spiritual aspects of your life that you should manifest or make real on a daily basis: compassion and peace. Because emotions used correctly – even with people you do not agree with, you do not like, people who would never seem to become your friend, those who do something to you or your family that you do not like – will demonstrate God to them. No matter how people treat us, if we will just use our God-given emotions the way He wants, Jesus will be seen and our actions will deeply impact people's lives.

When you display and live out a life of compassion and peace something will shift in a relationship. Rather than go at it with people, instead let the argument go or release people to have the freedom to believe in a different way. Suddenly something will shift in the relationship. God then has the opportunity to move in someone's life whether it is seen in that moment or not.

No matter what someone says about Jesus His emotions were constantly in play in His life. John 11:35 simply says, "Jesus wept." He was at the graveside of Lazarus and He was so overcome with love and emotion for His friend who had died and for all of the family members who were grieving, that He broke and wept. The family was saying "If you had only come sooner. If you had only been here you could have healed Lazarus." Jesus was totally God and totally man, yet the emotions He displayed were totally under control.

People talk about how Jesus saves us – Yeshua means Savior. He saved me from emotions controlling my life. As a child I would banter with people, argue with them and lose my temper easily. But God has saved me from my emotions controlling me like they would have if I had not let Him into my life. How I respond, react and view other people, just to see what God is doing in them in heaven and on earth is controlling emotions just like Jesus did. I do it a whole lot better today than I did while working as a Youth Pastor in my twenties. In those days my drive to accomplish my purpose and what I wanted to accomplish would at times run people over. Today when I see the young people of our congregation doing something that years ago I would have erupted and chewed them out for I shake my head and think "oh man, what a strange way to have to learn things." Jesus is teaching me to control my emotions.

Consider this question. Does it bother you that Jesus did not have to give His life the way He did? He had the choice. He didn't have to die the way He did. There are two or three times according to the Bible where Jesus tried to talk Father God out of it. "I don't want to do this, I don't want to go through this" Jesus said. But because of His commitment to Father God and His commitment to you, He went through everything He did at the end of His life and died on a cross. He knew what was going to come, the Bible says He knew the joy that was set before Him – but to get to that was going to be really, really hard. His flesh and His soul said "I don't want to do this. But Father if there is no other way, then I am going to do this." He said it in John chapter 12 and again in the Garden of Gethsemane where Jesus said "I don't want to drink this cup but if there's no other way I'll do what you want because Your will is what's important to Me."

That is how much He loves you. Please get that – that is how much He loves you. As the Son of God He was in heaven and decided He was going to come down here and live a life with people who do not always think right, who do not always get along with each other, who find the silliest things to get upset about, who will see one thing and believe Him with great faith and then the next day almost forget they had faith. Jesus decided He was going to come down here and He was going to live for them, and then He was going to die for them. What an incredible gift. In the midst of that was the ability to control His emotions and demonstrate Father God in every way. Jesus knew that the giving was more important than the pain that He was going to endure.

Jesus lived an abundant life while here on earth and so can we. Jesus said in John 10:10 that He came that we may have life and have it abundantly. Part of living life abundantly is making yourself enjoy the surprises in life. We know that Jesus said He did not know everything that was going to happen, so there were surprises in His life that he enjoyed, the hug of a little child, the smile of friends, even gifts that people must have given to Him. Let me challenge you to enjoy the surprises in your life and look at them as

God's blessings. When something happens and someone does something that surprises you simply say, "Thanks Lord!" When you receive something that may not be what you want, overcome your emotional response of being disappointed and show gratitude for it. Make yourself; make your emotions be grateful.

Do not fake your emotions. You literally can change your emotional response to something and be grateful for it. Jesus endured the cross knowing the joy that was set before Him. He controlled, perhaps even changed His emotional responses and ultimately was grateful for it. He did not fake it, He endured and changed it.

After years of trying to hide and deny a desire I have had because it might be considered prideful I realized reading the Bible that it is a good thing to want to be great in God's Kingdom. First because Jesus was great in God's Kingdom and I want to be like Jesus; then because Jesus gave us permission to be great in His Kingdom. He said in Matthew 20:26 that whoever wants to become great in His Kingdom will be a servant. Jesus gives anyone who wants permission to seek greatness in His Kingdom. Jesus was great in the Kingdom of God and I want to be like Jesus. It is not an issue of pride, it is not a bad thing – it is something Jesus gives permission to desire. Do you ever wonder where in our tradition we began to believe pride is always a factor in greatness? To be great like Jesus was in God's Kingdom, He said He didn't come to be served but to serve; we only need to be a servant of others. If we will serve others Jesus says we will be great – how simple is that?

Not only that, but it seems that God wants us to have more fun than most Christians want us to have. So, we should not allow our emotions to rob us of the fun that God intends us to have. My wife and I have enjoyed giving our children gifts as they have grown up. We enjoyed watching them play with the toys and wear the clothes. So if we enjoyed our children having fun with what we gave them, imagine how much Father God enjoys His children having fun with what He has given them. I believe that it is God's desire to bless His children and to express His love to us. And the more we become like Jesus, the more we will know we are living in God's perfect will for us. So rather than allow our emotions to control us, let's be like Jesus and allow Holy Spirit to fill us, to lead us, to guide and to demonstrate to others God's love.

Printed in the United States
208909BV00001B/53/P